GETTING READY TO TEACH SIX

M000100633

Kiriki de Diego Metzo

Photos by Bruce Hazelton

Illustrated by Dave McPeek

Melanie Wieland, Janice Gutierrez, Deanna Bonach

We warmly thank the community of Alta Vista Elementary School, Redondo Beach, California, especially Mr. Leonard Stoll, principal; Ms. Melanie Wieland, Mrs. Janice Gutierrez, and Mrs. Deanna Bonach, sixth-grade teachers; and students, parents, and caregivers of the sixth-grade classes; Ms. Simone Charles of Williams Elementary School, Hawthorne, CA; and Mrs. Judy Ciampa of Fern Avenue School, Torrance, CA.

Project Manager: Barbara G. Hoffman

Editor: Barbara G. Hoffman

Book Design: Anthony D. Paular

Cover Design: Anthony D. Paular

Pre-Press Production: Daniel Willits and Randy Shinsato

TABLE OF CONTENTS

Let us put our minds together and see what life we can make for our children.

—Tatanba Iotanko (Sitting Bull) 1877

CHAPTER ONE: INTRODUCTION

PROLOGUE

Just as you are about to meet your first sixth grade, you are meeting me for the first time, so I'd like to tell you a bit about myself. In 1998, I retired from teaching after thirty years in the classroom and ten years tutoring children with learning difficulties. Writing this book has allowed me the opportunity to gather my experiences together and pass them on to others. It has been an interesting process, and a wonderful way to review my work. I hope my experiences and plans will be of help to you in the sixth grade.

To begin, I started cleaning out my recipe files the other day, throwing away recipes from newspapers that were fun to read but that would probably never make it to my table. In the collection of clippings I came across a piece of school notebook paper, torn sloppily from a pad covered with notes to motivate a spelling story and descriptions of pieces at a museum I wanted my class to observe on an upcoming trip. There weren't any ingredients on the sheet for a wonderful recipe or instructions for mixing, just my ideas for a class museum trip and a spelling test tucked away with recipes for the staff of life and other nutrients. I had obviously let my lives cross over—food for the body and food for the mind. What follows is my recipe for your first year of teaching sixth grade. Add your own ingredients and adjust seasonings to your taste.

1

Learning and teaching do not take place in a vacuum; the stuff of the classroom should not be completely separated and unrelated to the life of the student or to that of the teacher. Part of a teacher's mission is to instill this idea in students. Their learning is a part of their lives, the curriculum isn't dreamed up to keep them from playing outside, rather to help them enjoy that play more.

I feel that one of a teacher's goals is to sensitize children to the learning that can be realized from all that's around them: parents, city streets, woods, subways, neighbors, books, movies and TV, libraries, museums, walks alone, and talks with friends.

Your role as the teacher is specialized. The three R's must be secured, mechanics of writing and arithmetic well-in-place to facilitate getting ideas on paper and working out problems. But, don't overlook the opportunity to use ideas that happen in one area inspire another in your life. Remember my beginning lesson plan in the recipe file. Let the opportunities presented to you inspire you and your students as well.

THE SIXTH GRADER

A typical sixth grader probably does not exist. The word that comes to mind when I picture one of my classes is of a motley crew, a most heterogeneous group in physical size and emotional maturity. A great variety in both is the norm. Yet there is something that pulls sixth graders together. Between the old "tens" and young "twelves" and the more numerous "elevens" there seems to be a combining quality, regardless of age, that makes them focus on the work at hand. They are aware, more than younger students, that this is an important year in school. The work at hand is interesting, and it will have an importance in their future school lives. School is important to the sixth grader for sports, intellectual stimulation, and as a social world.

Sixth graders are independent as human beings and responsible for their work and their behavior.

> **Learning is discovering that something is possible.**
> —Fritz Perls, "Omni", November 1979

They are concerned with fairness to themselves and to those in their peer groups. Yet, as I said in the beginning, they are a motley group and in your grade there will be students who must be reminded constantly about their homework and rules of the classroom. Some of them may act more like fourth graders than sixth graders. However, by the end of the year they will all have grown into students who can be expected to complete assignments on their own and on schedule. They will be ready to take their place in the upper grades.

Peer respect and recognition is very important and judgements of classmates can be devastating. A small group of girls can often be hurtful to others outside their own group. They use language to belittle and make fun of outsiders to their own group. This can be very disruptive to the focus of the entire class and the atmosphere in the room. It is important to be on the lookout for cliques of any kind and to refocus their attention.

The social dynamics of the group are often created by pressures outside the classroom: expectations at home and/or from friends, and very strong pressures from the commercial world. Advertising which suggests what brand to wear has a great influence over this age group. You can get help in avoiding some of this negative force in the classroom by interesting parents in class activities and social goals for the group at Back-to-School Night (see page 82).

Academically the sixth grade student has the basics: they read, know the multiplication tables, and the spelling rules. They have had experience organizing their ideas into stories and reports, and solving problems that use numbers and measurements. In your class they will go on to more difficult problems and higher level thinking.

CURRICULUM OVERVIEW FOR SIXTH GRADE

In your state, county, or city there is, no doubt, a prescribed curricula for each grade whether you teach in a public, independent, or parochial school. However, much of the curricula for sixth grade is review, though each concept previously learned or skill taught is expanded to provide students with a greater depth of understanding.

This section is presented in alphabetical order by content area. The sequence is Language Arts, Mathematics, Multicultural Education, Physical Education, Science and Health, Social Studies, Technology, and Visual and Performing Arts (which includes Music).

In this overview section you will read about the concepts that are to be addressed in sixth grade. In Chapter Two—Bringing the Curriculum to Life—you will find in each content area a list of skills for that subject generally accepted as appropriate for sixth grade. After the lists of skills, you will find activities that you can use to teach the skills or ways to incorporate them into your classroom.

The content and curriculum information presented in this book is provided as a reference. It is not intended to replace your school or district's course of study or curriculum guides. As additional references, you should read the standards published by national teacher organizations such as the National Council of Teachers of Mathematics or the National Council of Teachers of English. Your school or district resource centers will probably have copies of these documents you can use as references.

Parts of the curriculum sections of this book are based on the Standards of the National Council of the Teachers of Mathematics, the National Council of the Teachers of English, and the National Research Council of the National Academy of Sciences. Other references used are state frameworks and school district curricula from Illinois, California, Nebraska, Massachusetts, Washington, and New York.

Language Arts

Language Arts is a broad area of the curriculum which includes reading, writing, listening, and speaking. Through each of these processes, students express what they know, what they think and what they value about the world. They make connections between information they know and information they don't know.

Your school or district may have adopted textbooks or other language arts programs that include grammar, spelling, activity, and workbooks, or there may be specific guidelines you are expected to follow. Check with the curriculum coordinator or principal at your school before the school year begins.

3

Concepts

- Language is used to communicate ideas across time and space.

- Language allows us to express our life experiences, to give names and labels to what we know and value, and to better understand and share ourselves with others.

- Comprehension and critical thinking are constructed personally as we build new knowledge, make decisions, and solve problems based on that knowledge.

- How language is used shapes the course of events. Science, major conflicts, and technology are major sources of new vocabulary.

Three components are important to developing the art of language in your classroom. The first is the use of literature, the second is an emphasis on writing as a process, and the third is easy access to many books and other educational media.

Literature, the first component, creates a bridge between the "real world" and your classroom, and between different curricular areas. In addition to making information interesting and accessible, literature is pleasurable to read.

The second component, writing, is an essential part of language development. The process of speech-to-print includes several stages—prewriting, drafting, receiving responses, revising, editing, and in many cases postwriting. Through the writing process students develop their writing and related skills. They also improve their spoken language because discussing their work and the work of others is a good way to learn about giving and receiving constructive criticism.

The third important component of developing the art of language in your classroom, is the use of library media resources. Your students should have regular access to a variety of materials from which they can select according to their own interests. You will need to develop a classroom library as well as use the resources of the school and local public libraries.

Students need more than facts. They need to understand the relationships between "facts" and whose interests certain "facts" serve. They need to question the validity of the "facts," to ask questions such as "why" and "how." They need to know how to find information, to solve problems, to express themselves in oral and written language so their opinions can be shared with, and have an influence on, broader society. It is only through such an approach that students can construct their own beliefs, their own knowledge.

—Bob Peterson "What Should Children Learn?: A Teacher Looks at E.D. Hirsch" in Rethinking Schools An Agenda for Change

Mathematics

- "Knowing" mathematics is "doing" mathematics. A person gathers, discovers, or creates knowledge in the course of some purposeful activity.

- Mathematics is a foundation discipline for other disciplines. Mathematical models, structures, and simulations are applicable to many disciplines.

- Mathematics is growing and changing. All students need mathematics to be productive citizens of the 21st-century.

In sixth grade, students apply mathematical skills to real-life problems.. They can use appropriate mathematical vocabulary to discuss ratio and proportion, probability, and simple equations. They understand the need to analyze and assess data and information.

Concepts

- Precise statements about what is known allow conjectures and conclusions to be examined logically.

- A series of logical arguments can be used to reach a valid conclusion when based on certain premises.

- Real objects and abstract shapes have one-, two-, and/or three-dimensional features which can be examined, compared, and analyzed.

- Geometric shapes have specific attributes and properties by which they are identified, classified, and named.

- Geometric shapes can be described in terms of their relationships (relative size, position, congruence, and similarity) with other shapes.

- We can attach a number to a quantity using a unit which is chosen according to the properties of the quantity to be measured.

- Selection of an appropriate measuring tool requires considering the size of what is to be measured and the use of the measure.

- Measurement is approximate because of the limitations of the ability to read a measuring instrument and the precision of the measuring instrument; the more accuracy you need, the smaller unit you need.

- Identifying the rule used to generate a pattern enables one to extend the pattern indefinitely.

- A functional relationship between two quantities indicates that the value of the first quantity determines the corresponding value of the second.

- The same patterns can emerge from a variety of settings.

- Questions that cannot be answered by direct observation can be assessed often by gathering data that often generates additional questions.

- Data can be gathered about every member of a group, or a representative sample from that group can be used.

- Data can be organized, represented, and summarized in a variety of ways.

- Inference made from a set of data can be invalid due to one or more reasons.

- Various strategies can be used to find out why some outcomes are more likely than others.

- A set of numerical relationships can be expressed through the use of variables.

- An equality relationship between two quantities remains true as long as the same change is made to both quantities.

- The properties of operations on variables are the same as the properties of operations on numbers.

- Numbers can be used to describe quantities and relationships between quantities.

- Any number can be described in terms of how many of each group there are in a series of groups and each group in the series is a fixed multiple (the base of the place value system) of the next smaller group.

- The four basic operations are related to one another and are used to obtain numerical information.

- The degree of precision needed in calculating a number depends on how the results will be used.

Multicultural

Multicultural Education is an interdisciplinary subject. It should be a part of the everyday curriculum. The concepts can be included in any lesson that you present. Through art, music, dance, language arts, and social science, students learn about different cultures, and learn to become increasingly aware of the culture and heritage of the country in which they live. The goal is to help students develop positive attitudes about themselves and other cultures. Through an anti-biased curriculum the students will learn to appreciate, respect, and value differences.

Physical Education

In sixth grade most students have mastered the basic locomotor skills.

Concepts

- **Motor Skills**—There are safe ways to catch balls. Practice throwing at targets increases hand-eye coordination. There are correct positions for square dancing.

- **Physical Fitness**—The body is affected by exercise, fatigue, illness, relaxation, and stress. Physical fitness can be described and explained in a variety of ways. Personal exercise programs can be designed to suit particular needs.

- **Self-Image**—Goal setting is important to those who desire to achieve. Achieving success requires practice, and the potential for success is constant. Success is not permanent, nor is failure.

- **Social Behavior**—Recognizing others for their efforts and accomplishments is a positive practice. Errors happen every day and should be tolerated between group members. Team leadership roles are valuable experiences.

- **Recreation**—Participation in recreational activities is revitalizing. A wide variety of activities promotes the development of many skills. There are many recreational activities available in the community.

> **We are going to have to find ways of organizing ourselves cooperatively, sanely, scientifically, harmonically and in regenerative spontaneity with the rest of humanity around earth . . . We are not going to be able to operate our spaceship earth successfully nor for much longer unless we see it as a whole spaceship and our fate as common. It has to be everybody or nobody.**
>
> **—Buckminster Fuller**

Science and Health

Science Concepts

Most state education standards and frameworks are written based on the National Science Education Standards (NSES). The NSES presents its content standards by grade ranges, K-4, 5-8, and 9-12. Consequently, specific sixth-grade science study topics vary considerably from state to state and district to district. The NSES 5-8 content standards published in 1996 follow. The science curriculum of your school or district will most likely be written to reflect these content standards.

Unifying Concepts and Processes
- Systems, order, and organization
- Evidence, models, and explanation
- Change, constancy, and measurement
- Evolution and equilibrium
- Form and function

Science as Inquiry
- Abilities necessary to do scientific inquiry
- Understandings about scientific inquiry

Physical Science
- Properties and changes of properties in matter
- Motions and forces
- Transfer of energy

Life Science
- Structure and function in living systems
- Reproduction and heredity
- Regulation and behavior
- Populations and ecosystems
- Diversity and adaptations of organisms

Earth and Space Science
- Structure of the earth system
- Earth's history
- Earth in the solar system

Science and Technology
- Abilities of technological design
- Understanding about science and technology

Science in Personal and Social Perspective
- Personal health
- Populations, resources, and environments
- Natural hazards
- Risks and benefits
- Science and technology in society

History and Nature of Science
- Science as a human endeavor
- Nature of scientific knowledge
- Historical perspectives

Sample Curriculum

Below is a sample curriculum that reflects topics frequently presented in sixth grade.

Life Science

- The cell is basic to most living organisms and related to tissues, organs, and body systems that carry essential functions.

- Genes are materials located in the chromosomes in cell nuclei and determine the characteristics of organisms.

- Most animals reproduce sexually when an egg and sperm unite.

- Photosynthesis enables plants to absorb sunlight and produce their own food.

- Protists may be either beneficial or harmful. Their control involves scientific applications, public policy, and personal behavior.

- An ecosystem consists of a community of living organisms interacting with each other and the environment.

- A population consists of one species that lives in a limited area. Populations may become endangered and species may become extinct.

- Fossils are formed in many ways. Fossil remains indicate that many species have become extinct and new species have come into being over geologic time.

Physical Science

- Matter has mass/weight and occupies space.

- Individual atoms, the building blocks of all matter, are in constant motion.

- Atoms which have a neutral charge are made up of even smaller particles: electrons, protons, and neutrons.

- Energy sources can be traced back to the sun's energy and are either renewable or nonrenewable.

- Elements are the fundamental building blocks.

> The world looks so different after learning science.
>
> For example, trees are made of air, primarily. When they are burned, they go back to air, and in the flaming heat is released the flaming heat of the sun which was bound in to convert the air into tree. [A]nd in the ash is the small remnant of the part which did not come from air, that came from the solid earth, instead.
>
> These are beautiful things, and the content of science is wonderfully full of them. They are very inspiring, and they can be used to inspire others.
>
> —Richard Feynman

- Energy cannot be created or destroyed but can be transferred from one object to another or changed from one form to another.

- A magnetic field produces an electric current in a conductor that moves through the magnetic field. An electric current moving through a conductor produces a magnetic field around that conductor.

- A static electric charge may be produced on objects rubbed together. There are two kinds of electric charges, positive and negative. Like charges repel and unlike charges attract each other.

- Light travels very rapidly in straight lines from its source and may be reflected, refracted, or absorbed.

- Concave mirrors can focus light by reflection; convex lenses can focus light by refraction.

- Visible light is a part of the electromagnetic spectrum of energy moving through space.

- Heat transfer can be accomplished by conduction, convection, and radiation.

Earth Science

- The sun is the center of the solar system. It is a massive sphere of hydrogen and helium that releases energy.

- The relationship between the earth and sun affects daily, seasonal, and annual changes.

- The atmosphere affects the amount of solar energy reaching earth.

- Astronomers use instruments to study constellations, galaxies, and celestial changes. Specific star characteristics can be determined from starlight.

- Earthquakes release large amounts of energy and change land forms.

Health Concepts

The focus of the health curriculum in sixth grade is on students learning to be self-directive and to deal assertively with peer and media pressures to experiment with harmful substances or engage in other risk-taking behavior.

- It's better to be well than ill. Long-term health and well-being requires an investment of time and caring for oneself. A balanced combination of physical activities, rest, recreation, and adequate diet contributes to fitness and cardiovascular health.

- Families take different forms. Each member affects the health of the others. Heredity and environment influence the development of living organisms. Understanding human growth and development through the life cycle leads to an appreciation of oneself and others. The capacity to adjust to, understand, and respect others will enhance one's interpersonal relationships.

- Daily food intake affects our personal health. Food choice is affected by life style, peers, and family economics.

- Making decisions is a process that helps reduce stress and anxiety, helps one gain self-respect, and obtain personal satisfaction. Understanding and liking oneself, making friends, and getting along with others is essential to good mental health. Understanding and coping with emotions in an acceptable way is healthy, while unresolved conflicts cause stress and anxiety which is unhealthy.

- Some substances may be beneficial when used properly, but can disrupt normal body functions when misused. Drugs are substances that change the way the mind and body work. We can be pressured by the environment or by those around us to use substances, but the choice is ours.

- Many factors contribute to diseases. Our ability to control and prevent disease varies.

- Individuals are responsible for their own health and for knowing when to seek help from others. The community provides health-care resources. There are many careers in the field of health. A relationship exists between the quality of the environment and human health. We must work together to create and maintain a safe and healthful environment.

- Many accidents can be prevented. Each of us needs to be prepared to act effectively in times of emergency. Identifying and correcting potential hazards and safety can help reduce accidents and save lives.

Social Studies

The goal of a balanced elementary social studies program is to prepare students to participate in society with the knowledge, skills, and civic values that enable them to be actively and constructively involved. In sixth grade, most students study the role of ancient civilizations as the foundation of Western society. Students study the chronological development of ancient civilizations and the impact that geographic location had upon them. Students appreciate the achievements of ancient peoples and their contributions to modern civilizations in the areas of religion, ethics, technology, and government.

Social Studies is an interdisciplinary subject. Many social studies concepts and skills can be studied as part of your language arts, math, science, and arts programs, as well as a separate unit of study. You may also find that social studies provides you the framework through which to study language arts, mathematics, science, and the arts.

Concepts

- The chronology of the human story begins with prehistoric man and evolves through ancient civilizations that were the precursors to, and the roots of, Western societies.

- The ethical basis for Western thought came from the ancient societies' concepts of wisdom, righteousness, law, and justice.

- The environment and its resources determined where ancient settlements developed and affected the rise and fall of great civilizations.

- The contributions of the ancient civilizations in art, architecture, drama, and poetry lasted through the centuries and greatly influenced Western culture and present day life.

- The environment and life styles of prehistoric people resulted in a transition from hunter-gatherers to food producers.

- Ancient societies evolved across the whole of the ancient world and established the foundation for modern civilization. The Greek city-state provides a model of a transition from tyranny and oligarchy to an early form of democracy.

TECHNOLOGY

For purposes of this overview, technology is defined as the application of knowledge to manipulate tools, machines, materials, techniques, and technical systems to satisfy human needs and wants.

Technology can be divided into two sections. One is industrial technology which involves learning construction processes and skills using wood, paper, cardboard, and plastic.

The second section is computer technology which involves learning computer concepts and tools. This arena is changing as fast as computer technology is. States and school districts are developing their academic standards in this field as this book goes to press.

We the peoples of the United Nations, determined to save succeeding generations from the scourge of war, which twice in our lifetime has brought untold sorrow to mankind, and to reaffirm faith in fundamental human rights, in the dignity and worth of the human person, in the equal parts of men an women and of nations large and small . . . and for these ends to practice tolerance and live together in peace with one another as good neighbors . . . have resolved to combine our efforts to accomplish these aims.

—Preamble to the Charter of the United Nations

Visual and Performing Arts

Visual Arts

Concepts

- We are surrounded by images and events, natural and human-made, that have visual and tactile qualities. We can describe the world with images and symbols with visual and tactile qualities.

- Knowledge of art techniques can help us express and communicate our experiences through art. Originality and personal experience are important to visual expression. Visual arts media can be used to communicate feelings and ideas.

- Art has played an important role in every culture throughout history. Studying art can give us insight into other cultures. We can learn about our creative abilities through art. Clarifying our personal aesthetic values can help us appreciate the aesthetic values of others.

- Using objective criteria for analysis, interpretation, and judgment based on aesthetic values results in informed responses to art and improved art production.

Performing Arts

Most schools and districts require that students have one or more opportunities a year to perform before a large audience. This may take the form of an assembly or a recital. Check with your administrator or colleagues to find out the requirements at your school.

Music

The sixth-grade student enjoys singing. Group singing is particularly rewarding. Some of your sixth-grade boys' voices will begin to change. Singing in harmony can be developed into two- and three-part music.

Concepts

- Technology and the future are interrelated.

- The environment and the future are dependent upon the proper use of technology.

- Plans and drawings have standards: dimensions, depth, height, width, scale, and so on.

- Mental skills are related to job skills.

- A system and a process are needed for technology to be effective.

- All technology requires energy.

- Computers are important components and tools in our society.

Concepts

- Rhythm flows on a recurring steady beat divided into sets of accented and unaccented beats. The rhythm of the melody consists of longer and shorter sounds and silences. Meter is the organization of beats into groups of twos or threes. Syncopation is created by accenting unaccented beats. Several different rhythms may be performed at the same time. Changing note values changes the rhythm pattern.

- A melody is made up of tones with higher or lower pitches, that may change up or down or repeat. When a melody ends on the home tone a feeling of repose is created. Visual symbols can be used to show the relationships between tones. Tones in a melody may go up or down by a step (scale) or skip (chord). A scale is a specific consecutive arrangement of tones. Melodies may be repeated, beginning on different pitches and sung or played in a higher or lower key. Music can be tonal or multi-tonal.

- The basic form in music is the phrase or musical thought. Identical phrases or sections contribute to the unity of a composition. A song or other composition may have an introduction, interlude, and a coda. Phrases may be partly the same or partly different. Contrasting phrases provide variety in compositions. A composition with two sections is called a two-part or binary form. A composition with three sections, the last a repeat of the first, is called three-part or ternary form (ABA). In rondo form the initial section (A) of a composition alternates with contrasting sections (ABACA). Theme and variation form consists of a melody followed by several restatements with alterations or changes. The *sonata allegro* form results when a composition is in extended ternary (three-part) form with two themes. A compound form contains various movements or parts. Musical compositions may be without form or structure such as *improvisation* and *aleatoric* music (music played at random).

- Songs can be performed with or without accompaniment. Harmony is created when two or more tones are sounded at the same time. Combining melodies results in a harmonic texture called polyphony (ostinato, countermelody, round, canon). A musical composition may be either major or minor depending on its melody or harmony. A chord consists of three or more tones sounded simultaneously. Harmony may apply to successions of chords. The tonic or I (one) chord creates a feeling of resolution or repose. The dominant or V (five) and the subdominant or IV (four) are active chords needing resolution when compared to the tonic chord. Musical texture results from combining melodic and harmonic elements.

- Sound is produced in diverse ways and can be modified. Tempo is relative rather than absolute. Music can move in a fast or slow tempo. Dynamics in music can be louder or softer. Changes of tempo and dynamics provide a source of variety and expressive meaning in a composition. Characteristic qualities of sounds are determined by the types of voices or instruments which produce them (timbre). Various combinations of musical elements result in different *styles* of music.

- Musicians reflect and interpret their times, values, cultures, and experiences.

- Music has a cultural and historical context.

- Music has made unique contributions to civilization that can be studied.

> **Music has always had its own syntax, its own vocabulary and symbolic means. Indeed, it is with mathematics the principal language of the mind when the mind is in a condition of non-verbal feeling.**
>
> **—George Steiner, Language and Silence, 1958**

CHAPTER TWO: BRINGING THE CURRICULUM TO LIFE

LESSON PLANNING

Lesson planning is crucial to effectively organize your instruction. Some schools and districts require you to follow the teachers' manuals of commercial textbook series. If you are not required to do this you will be responsible for planning your instructional year. There are as many ways to plan as there are teachers—there is no one "right" way. The following is a guide.

Planning your program of instruction is like planning a dinner party. Before you plan a dinner party, you already know certain things. You know how many people you have invited and where you're going to hold the party. You have a certain time frame in mind, and you know that you are going to serve dinner.

First you must decide the presentation of your meal: will it be formal or informal? Sit-down dinner or buffet? Based on that decision you decide what the menu of your meal will be—a meal traditional to your family and culture, or an ethnic meal? Do you want each food course to be completely different, or do you want the meal to have some unifying elements?

When you know the menu, you find the recipes, and review the ingredients and how to prepare them. You schedule your purchases and preparation time. Once the dinner is prepared you assess your results by tasting what you prepare, watching people eat the meal, and seeing what is left over.

Long-Term Planning

You can think of lesson planning in the same way as planning the dinner party. You know how many students you have, you know where you are going to teach them, and you know you are going to teach them the content and skills your school or district requires over the the year. (You will find this information in your school or district's curriculum guide or course of study. Ask your administrator for a copy of the curricular requirements as soon as you can.) You also know that you need to organize all the information you must teach into a time frame—the school year.

Think about the concepts you want to teach over the next term. Decide which areas of study will provide good frameworks for these concepts. Decide what kinds of projects (the *menu*) will give your students many opportunities to learn and practice their learning. Projects can include anything from reading thirty pages in the textbook to converting your classroom into a medieval inn. Create, select, or choose activities (*recipes*) that will support the themes and promote the learning and practice of skills (*ingredients*).

Decide how many weeks (or days) you will need to accomplish your projects. Make a calendar or time-line of the unit.

Now that you know **what** you want to accomplish you need to plan **how** you will accomplish your long-term plans. Your weekly and daily lesson plans are the way to organize your activities (*recipes*) into a feasible schedule.

Plan Book

A lesson-plan book will be a useful purchase if your school or district does not provide one. There are many varieties from which to choose, from the most basic notebook-sized with gridded pages to large plan books that include lesson plan ideas.

Weekly Plans

Make detailed plans and schedule your instruction a week in advance. Include any regular or unusual events in the plan, such as school assemblies, class visitors, library visits, or short school days. Decide what lessons you want to include in the week and fit them into your schedule.

Daily Plans

For your daily plans you will want to balance activities that require sitting with activities where your students can move around. To begin the year you should assume that 35 minutes is long enough to require a student to stay focused on the same thing. As they develop, and you get to know them better, you will find what length of time works best for your students. You will also discover exactly what a "wide range of abilities" means. Some students can do whatever you ask them to do, well, in less than half the time that other students require. Plan activities or extra projects to engage these students when they have finished required work. In addition, as you are planning, you may want to decide what homework activities to assign.

Planning a Lesson

Decide what the focus or purpose of the lesson is. It should be clearly stated, because the clearer your purpose, the easier to design a lesson that accomplishes the purpose. Some examples of purposes follow.

- The purpose of this activity is to compare graphically the geologic age of the earth with the length of time human life has been on the planet.

- The purpose of this activity is to compute distances between cities on a map using the mileage scale.

List the materials that will be needed. If you need to order any supplies or get other items, you can do so in advance.

Plan the introduction to your lesson to give students background knowledge that will help them understand the new information. Literature, songs, and pictures can build background knowledge and motivate your students.

Plan exactly what you are going to do and how you are going to do it. Walk through the procedure in your head. If the lesson involves following directions and/or making something, do the activity yourself before you present it to your class. This will help you identify trouble spots. It is much easier to make necessary adjustments before you present it to a group of excited sixth graders.

After you present the lesson your students should have time to work independently on the skill you have presented. This gives them the practice necessary to learn it. You may wish to have the students work on the skill in small groups.

Planning for Assessment

The final element to consider is how to assess the effectiveness of the lesson. Use informal observations of students involved in the independent activity planned for the lesson combined with formal checks of the work. For more information on record keeping, see page 73.

Thinking through and planning each lesson is essential to your becoming the most effective teacher you can be.

USING THEMES

Themes are big ideas, larger than facts, concepts, and skills. Using a theme allows you to integrate the various content areas. It will provide you with a framework to guide you in the design and development of your instructional program. A theme provides you a way to make words and abstract ideas concrete, and to help your students see how ideas relate to other ideas and to their own experiences.

Themes link concepts and skills for your students. As you present new lessons framed in the context of your thematic unit, students can easily add the new information to the knowledge they already have. It is easier for students to learn skills, because they have knowledge and experience which create a context within which to apply the skills. In sixth grade, the themes can be abstract ideas such as "Integrity," "Courage," or "Spirits of Adventure."

As you get familiar with the curriculum, you will find that your instructional program grows out of it—naturally organizing itself into themes that reflect your interests. The more interested you are in what you are doing, the better you will do it, and you will see your kids turn on to learning.

LANGUAGE ARTS

Skills

- Compare and contrast information about a topic found in textbooks with that found in books and other media. Discuss why there may be differences (for example, poor research, poor reporting, poor writing styles, limited understanding of what the data actually mean, and so on).

- While giving an oral presentation use vocal pitch, intonation, stress, volume, and phrasing appropriate for the presentation and for the listening audience.

- Informally participate in pre-writing efforts of others and respond to peers' first-draft writing efforts.

- Participate in small groups to discuss alternative ways or formats in which each student writers' first-draft ideas or information might be stated differently.

- Use a variety of formats, both print and media, for documenting and debriefing shared classroom or home study activities.

- Use a range of graphic organizers to display and classify information, to analyze data, and to evaluate cause and effect.

- Recognize, develop, and deliver different kinds of speeches using descriptive language. These speeches may include testimonials, political speeches, bandwagon and propaganda speeches and speeches containing generalities.

- Persuade an audience, orally and in writing, that self or peers are qualified for service as a class or school leader. Create campaign posters and flyers.

- Tell or write an autobiographical incident providing all specific information (who, what, when, where, why, and how). State why the selected event is personally significant.

- Recognize and develop generalizations about literary, media, or content-area information such as news stories, magazine articles, political cartoons, letters to the editor, and weather reports from different regions of the world.

- Recognize and discuss obvious bias, propaganda, and semantic slantings found in different genres of text, in the media, and in government documents from different historical periods. Discuss and write about cause and effect.

- Use firsthand information such as interviews, surveys, and questionnaires to create an oral history about another person. Use graphics or other media to enhance the presentation.

- Summarize a book and discuss its format, how the author developed character, its plot design and related conflicts, and the major and minor themes.

- Evaluate a work of art, a section of text with photographs or illustrations on the same page or pages, a movie or video, or a familiar product such as a toy, an article of clothing, or an electronic item. Use details to support the evaluation.

> The function of thinking is not just solving an actual problem but discovering, envisaging, going into deeper questions. Often in great discoveries the most important thing is that a certain question is found. Envisaging, putting the productive question is often a more important, often a greater achievement than solution of a set question.
>
> —M. Wertheimer, Productive Thinking, 1945

• Write a personal opinion stating the most significant aspect of an activity or local event observed firsthand. Support why it is considered the most significant aspect.

The basis of the sixth-grade curriculum is to strengthen the verbal and written communication skills so that each student can express his or her ideas in a creative or factual form. Listening critically is, I think, the most difficult skill that sixth-grade students must acquire. This is a difficult task because not everything that is said in the classroom is of equal interest or importance. Everyone, teachers and students, has off days. So, providing a classroom atmosphere which gives all participants in the class a feeling that what they say is worthy of an ear is very important. You, the teacher, do this by listening and responding to what anyone says with a nod or comment, waiting for the proper time for criticism, either good or bad. You provide a sense that this classroom is a safe place to try out a new idea. Eye contact with the speaker is an important part of listening.

Writing enables people to preserve their thoughts and keep them over generations. Because words can be strung together in an endless line, punctuation is an important skill that needs to be reviewed and exercised. Sixth graders should be able to organize their writing in paragraphs and recognize sentence fragments and run-ons. Writing every day in the classroom or for homework should be part of the weekly schedule. Assigning different kinds of writing: editorial, personal, descriptive, narrative, and poetic should give the student an idea of the range of possibilities open to express their feelings and opinions. Students should be able to write a straight narrative or one with dialogue; use the essay form for papers in science, social studies or language arts; organize a report on a subject with several sub-headings; and experiment with one or two forms of poetry.

The sixth-grade reader should be able to discuss the character of the protagonists, the conflict or crisis of a story, and the conclusion or moral. Students should be able to recognize and discuss written work according to genre and style.

Reading and writing, quite simply, are the most important skills that we learn. They enable us to communicate with others and are necessary to accomplish much of what we do every day, in school and out. Usually the sixth-grade student, though he or she may not be a dedicated and/or proficient reader, has the necessary decoding skills. But even though they know the code, some of the students haven't become readers. So this is the challenge to the sixth-grade teacher: help students become aware of the world of the imagination that is found in books. The best way to accomplish this is to offer students a great list of wonderful books that includes books of all styles that can be read by the whole class or in small groups, and that will stimulate discussion and interest on the part of the students.

17

In planning a reading program for my Language Arts class, I would use contemporary authors, picking books with a similar theme. The focus on a similar topic shows students how different authors can approach the same subject. Some more successfully than others, naturally, which then stimulates a good discussion about why one book was more successful than the other.

The historical novel is an interesting genre to explore with your class. There are wonderful stories about the eras and events that sixth graders study. Because the heroes of the stories are close in age to the readers, the historical period comes alive with people like themselves, but in a different setting and a different time. The novels are ways to time travel and learn interesting facts about the lives of young teens through the ages to complement or supplement the social studies material with which you are working.

I included a period called Silent Sustained Reading (SSR) in my schedule. This 15-minute period of the day was devoted to reading. Everyone read, including me. My idea and hope was that it would begin to instill the habit of reading in the students and that, even if they had finished an assigned story, they would begin another on their own. The only rule was that students should read a book, not a magazine, catalogue or comic, but a novel, collection of short stories, even poetry. The book could be one that had been assigned. Some teachers may find that stimulating a student to read even a comic book is a great achievement. Keep your expectations high, but adjust how high "high" is, based on the expertise of your students.

Recommended Reading

Assign writers whose work comes under the category *Young Adult Literature.* They are a wonderful group of authors! Because they are contemporary, they know the world of young people today. Their writing captures the pace of today's life and therefore the interest and imagination of sixth-grade readers.

Gary Paulsen, a writer who appeals to that most difficult of student readers, boys, has this to say about his writing and why he doesn't write for adults. "Teenagers are still new, young, still fresh and willing to take ideas." About his book *Soldier's Heart* (Doubleday, 1998) he adds, the story doesn't make "war some kind of pap that's not true; it's what it's really like." His stories are strong, well-told, honest, adventurous, sometimes very funny, and **short**. The **short** may be why boys like them.

I'm including a list of books that I've found to have been successful over a number of years. I'm sure some titles are very familiar. I hope that some will be new to you and prove to be interesting reading to you and your students.

> **The love of learning, the sequestered nooks.**
> **And all the sweet serenity of books.**
>
> —Henry Wadsworth Longfellow

Families

Judie Angell, *Tina Gogo* (Laurelleaf, 1978). This story tells of a young girl who is hard to befriend because she lies.

Betsy Byars, *The Not Just Anybody Family* (BDD Books, 1987). The everyday lives of three children in the Blossom family whose adventures are told in a spirited way. Their grandfather is in charge when their mother is away working in the rodeo.

Other Books by Betsy Byars—*A Blossom Promise* (BDD Books, 1989), *The Blossoms Meet the Vulture Lady* (BDD Books, 1987), *Wanted–Mud Blossom* (Delacorte, 1991) are three more stories about the Blossoms. They are very entertaining tales! *The Pinballs* (Harper Collins, 1977). This book is about more serious difficulties in a non-traditional family, but told with great sensitivity by Ms. Byars.

Paula Fox, *Lily and the Lost Boy* (Orchard Books Watts, 1987). Set on a Greek isle, Lily and her brother try to find adventure during their father's sabbatical. An adventure becomes a tragedy when they meet another American boy, Jack. Though set in modern Greece, the reader, through the protagonists, explores antiquities that still exist on the island and experiences the rural life on the island that is not quite as up-to-date as home in America.

Katherine Paterson, *The Great Gilly Hopkins* (Trophy Books, 1987). A very powerful story of a foster child's meeting with her real mother. This is a must read!

Cynthia Voigt, *A Solitary Blue* (Scholastic, 1993). A young boy accepts, with pain, the feelings of his mother. Similar to Gilly but the protagonist is male and the style is very different. Good for comparing.

Historical Stories

Marguerite de Angeli, *The Door in the Wall* (Doubleday, 1989). In plague-ridden medieval London a young boy is deserted by his caretakers. He reunites with his father in time to take part in a battle with the Welsh and save the day.

Karen Cushman, *Catherine, Called Birdy* (Trophy, 1995). A willful young girl asserts her right to choose her own husband in 13th-century Britain.

Peter Dickinson, *The Dancing Bear* (Yearling, 1972). In the sixth century, Rome has fallen and Europe has been invaded by barbarians, so a slave, the bear he tends, and a holy man go to rescue the daughter of Lord Celsus of Byzantium. The story is a wonderful combination of early Christian theology, history, and true adventure. It is for mature readers.

Elizabeth J. Gray, *Adam of the Road* (Puffin, 1987). This book tells the story of a young minstrel in 13th-century Britain making his way from St. Alban Abbey to London to Oxford in search of his father and his stolen dog.

E. L. Konigsburg, *A Proud Taste for Scarlet and Miniver* (BDD Books, 1985). The author, through Eleanor of Aquitaine, tells the queen's history as she waits to see if her husband, Henry II, will arrive in heaven. She visits with her mother-in-law, Queen Maud, and Abbot Suger as they peer out at the sky from a cloud and recall past events. The reader has to decide if Henry II makes it or not.

19

Mary Stolz, *Bartholomew Fair*, (Beechtree Bks, 1990). A wonderful tale of six people from very different walks of life who go to Bartholomew Fair on the same day in 1597. It is a mystery since not all of them get home.

Rosemary Sutcliff, *Eagle of the Ninth* (FS & G, 1993). Using the fact that in 117 AD a Roman Legion marched north from York to drive out the rebellious tribes living there, Ms. Sutcliff writes a wonderful tale of Marcus Aquila, son of the legion commander. The young man hopes to discover what happened to the Legion, recover its crest, and also his father's honor.

Rosemary Sutcliff, *The Shining Company* (FS & G, 1992). This time in seventh-century Britain, Ms. Sutcliff recounts the adventures of a young man, Proper, who goes to fight the invading Saxons.

Henry Winterfeld, *Detectives in Togas* and *Mystery of the Roman Ransom* (both books - Harcourt Brace, 1990). Two wonderful stories, full of details of life in Rome at the beginning of the Empire, in which a group of school boys solves important mysteries. The boys are greatly helped in finding the solutions by their stern teacher, Xantippus.

For retelling of the works of Homer I recommend Padraic Colum's *The Golden Fleece and the Heroes Who Lived Before Achilles* (Macmillan, 1983), *The Children's Homer: The Adventures of Odysseus and The Tale of Troy* (Macmillan, 1982), and the books of Will and Mary Osborne or Bernard Evslin for reading the stories of the Greek & Roman gods that are part of our literary heritage. Ingri and Edgar d'Aulaire *D'Aulaire's Book of Greek Myths* (Doubleday, 1962) is a standard that may have been read to your students by their teachers and parents when they were very young. Knowing these stories well will give students a basis from which to compare the similarities and differences of myths and tales of other cultures and other times.

> **Literature is a transmission of power. Text books and treatises, dictionaries and encyclopedias, manuals and books of instructions—they are communications; but literature is a power line, and the motor, mark you, is the reader.**
>
> **—Charles P. Curtis, <u>A Commonplace Book</u>, 1957**

Others

Gary Paulsen has a whole shelf of books that are excellent. His story, *Woodsong* (Puffin, 1991), in which he writes of his running the Iditarod is wonderful. Laurence Yep's, *Dragon's Gate* (Trophy, 1995), is a powerful story of the building of the railroad and the use of Chinese labor. He also writes of life in China at the time explaining why so many wanted to emigrate. Jeanne Wabatsulo Houston and her husband, James D. Houston have written a story, *Farewell to Manzanar* (Bantam, 1983) about the internment of the Japanese in California during WWII. It is the story of Mrs. Houston's family and her experiences as a young person.

Elizabeth Spear is another great writer of historical fiction: *The Bronze Bow* (Sandpiper, 1973) takes place in Roman Palestine; *The Witch of Blackbird Pond* (BDD Books, 1978) is about making judgements without true information in early New England.

Shades of Gray by Carolyn Reeder (Avon, 1991) is an excellent book about taking sides in the Civil War which would probably be a good read with Mr. Paulsen's *Soldier's Heart* (Doubleday, 1998).

A last suggestion is the work of William Steig: *Dominic* (Sunburst, 1984) for language and delightful character puns, and *The Real Thief* (Sunburst, 1984) to foster thinking about owning up to what you do. Mr. Steig's drawings may put some students off and make them think of his work as juvenile, but his ideas and his vocabulary are not.

Many of these books are favorites of mine and of my students. I've learned that the writing of contemporary authors, those who write Young Adult Literature, is in tune with the way today's teenagers think. The language of the stories, whether the plots evolve in historic time or now, appeals to them. Students become excited by the work because they are able to relate to the people and events in the stories. Knowing more about the history of a period makes students understand and better enjoy the writings of Dickens, Robert Louis Stevenson, and Shakespeare when they are in high school.

Some of the books that I've mentioned have been dramatized on film or video. As a rule I haven't shown them to my students although we have discussed the dramatizations if a good number of the students have seen them. Often they will take issue with a film if they have really enjoyed the book. A discussion of film versus reading is appropriate to this age. My feeling is that their imaginations need exercising and creating the characters in their own minds is a way to do this.

Reading Goals

Reading goals for students is that they be able to identify plot, conflict, turning points, characters, genre of a literary work, and author's style. Present the ideas you want students to think about as they read, using the vocabulary you want them to use in their discussions. What's the plot? How does it begin? What's the crisis or conflict? Where does the turning point take place in the story? Who is the protagonist? Is there an antagonist? What genre does the literary work belong to? How would you characterize the style of the author? I suggest that the first book you assign be a short novel. Steig's *The Real Thief* (Sunburst, 1984) is a good example since it is a fast and easy read. Assign the story one day, and discuss it the next. After discussing the questions noted above, give a written test. The discussion will have given students a good idea of what is expected of them to express in written form about the story.

I've included a sample test for *The Real Thief,* to give you an idea how to reflect the goals of reading in a test format on page 26.

Writing Goals

Before giving a test, go over the goals for written work for the year. The sentence is a good place to begin. Sixth graders should know what a sentence is; they should be able to catch and correct incomplete sentences, and break up run-ons into two or more complete ideas. They should recognize verbs, nouns, adjectives and adverbs. The student should understand the role each part of speech takes in a sentence. One interesting thing about words is how they can change their part of speech and meaning by their role in a sentence. Is the word the subject or the action? Does it describe a person or place or how something is done in a sentence?

Spelling correctly is an ongoing goal during their schooling. Provide a weekly list of words and test for meaning, usage, part of speech and etymology. The most important thing will be students using the words they are learning in their writing and expressing their ideas in sentences.

On the spelling tests I designed I tried to use the spelling words in different ways to demonstrate how to use the words in sentences. I sometimes wrote the story in a different tense so that the spelling word would have to be changed to make it fit the story.

Tests of all kinds are ways to practice writing and develop skill in sentence structure and paragraphing. But it is confining and you want to have students experience many different kinds of writing. Journals are popular, but I've always felt that I was invading the students' space when I read their journals. However, daily writing doesn't have to be that personal. A journal can have stories, feelings about current affairs, or things happening in the school or classroom. The paragraph in the journal can be a basis for a longer piece. However, even their short work and rough drafts should be read and commented on. So you want to set up a system that allows you to read everything.

Organizing the Flow of Written Work so that You Don't Drown in it

If you have a class of 30 students, you want to organize your work so that you can read, comment and return the writing the next day or at the latest, the day after. When students don't get responses to their work in a reasonable time, their enthusiasm can wane.

Dividing the class into two groups, even three, is a solution. Stagger the nights that you hand out an assignment. For example, I will assign the written part of the social studies homework to ten students on Monday, make the same assignment to a different ten on Tuesday, and make the assignment to the third group on Wednesday.

Another solution is to have students edit each other's work before you see it. In a class just under 20, I've made copies of their work, masked the names, and handed out the work so that each student would edit someone else's paper. Having partners or a group of three or four is another way to do initial editing. Introduce the idea of the "Blue Pencil" but have them work on their own papers first before someone else blue-pencils their story. Using proofreaders' marks gives the correction process some panache. Editing and revising should become part of the writing process if your students aren't already doing them.

The Writing Process

- Prewriting—getting ideas on paper
- Drafting—rough draft stage
- Revising—reviewing and changing work
- Proofreading—correcting spelling, syntax, and mechanical errors
- Publishing,—creating the final copy
- Sharing—presenting the work

¶ Begin a new paragraph. Indent the paragraph.

∧ Insert a letter, word, phrase, or sentence.

⌃ Insert a comma.

⩔⩔ Insert quotation marks.

⊙ Insert a period.

ℐ Take out a letter, word, phrase, or sentence.

/ Change a capital letter to a small letter.

= Change a small letter to a capital letter.

(sp) Check the spelling of a word.

Reading Aloud

Opportunities for reading aloud to the class by you and your students should occur several times a week. Give students time to prepare the reading either in school or as homework. There will be students who love to read to the class and others who will not. Some students will not want to read aloud because of shyness. Some will have a real difficulty in getting the words out the way they see them on the page. Work with those who have difficulty, one-to-one.

Since reading aloud is close to drama, perform scenes from class readings. Divide the class into groups of three or four students. Some rehearsal time is necessary whether in school or as homework. One group reads while the others watch. Having another group following the first with the same scene or one that comes next in the book can lead to a discussion of the different interpretations of the same characters in the different scenes.

At the outset, make it clear to students that criticism is a way to be helpful, not an opportunity to put someone or something down. If students are not responding constructively, stop the dramatizations immediately, explaining that students must not show disrespect for someone's work.

Sample Language Arts Tests

Vocabulary

The following are vocabulary words from *The Real Thief.* You could use them in the weekly spelling list or separately.

aghast, dastardly, doltish, domain, egress, fissure, halberd, irrational, nabob, obliterate, pliable, recluse, rubescent, salver, scrutinize, succulent

Spelling

The language test I've included on page 24 includes a beginning paragraph I wrote for the test. The students refer to the spelling list to find the words to write in the blanks. The same instructions would be used each week, with changes in the number of words used, or structures that complement particular grammatical lessons to review.

The opening paragraph provides the student with possibilities for a rather dramatic middle and end. Include review words to facilitate the drama.

Homophone/homonym Test

Include as part of your spelling curriculum, the homonyms/homophones that plague us all. It is a good class exercise to compile that list on the board at the beginning of the week and then include the words in pairs or triplets throughout the weekly tests. Have students make up paragraphs using several pairs as practice using the words. Challenge them to make up a story like the paragraph on page 24 using only homonyms in the blanks. If your students enjoy playing with words, they'll enjoy this activity! The homophone/homonym test on page 25 is an example of one way to test these words. You could also have students write sentences giving them a new (knew) list of homophones, or invent new puzzles to practice using the correct word. The list grows during the year since it is a fun group of words to play with. Practice with their, there, and they're and to, too, and two constantly.

Short Answer Test

I have included a short answer test on *The Real Thief* on page 26.

Answers to the Language Arts Tests

Language test page 24

1. soothing

2. punctuated

3. emerge

4. stifle

5. constant, continuous, or exhausting

Homophone/Homonym Test

page 25

1. fare, ferry

2. been, fair

3. there, two, council

4. hair, fairy, flower

5. hare, pair

6. flour, dough, pear

7. counsel, their

8. pare, hostel

9. tow, gate

10. toe, gait

11. vain, sew, vein

12. woe, hostile

13. boar, whoa

14. bore, sow, bean

15. doe, to, too

23

Language Test

Instructions: Using the new and review words for this week's test, fill in the blanks in the opening paragraph, name the parts of speech over the words you filled in, and finish the story. Use five other words from this week's list in your conclusion. You must name the part of speech over each word you use from the spelling list. You may change the form of the word to fit your story. If you use two different forms of a word, you may count it only once.

The (1)_____ quiet of Henry's morning sleep was suddenly (2)_____

by the loud ringing of a bell. "What is that sound?" wondered Henry. It was Saturday and he was

not ready to (3)_____ from his room, let alone his bed. The bell rang again. He

covered his head with the blanket to (4) _____ the (5)_____ clamor. Henry

had to do something!

The new words for the week were:				
monotonous	brawl	casual	originate	constant
punctuate (change tense)	excel	ravenous	exhaust	hardy
soothe (change form)	mediocre	stampede	veteran	realistic

Review for the week:	
apparel	emerge
continuous	sheathe
stifle	

_____

_____

_____

_____

_____

_____

_____

Teacher: The answers to this test are found on page 23.

FS122008 Getting Ready to Teach Sixth Grade

Name _____   Date _____

Homonyms or Homophones

Words that have the same sound but are spelled differently and have different meanings are called homonyms or homophones. When you hear the word in a spoken sentence you know what is meant, but you have to be careful when you're using them in your writing to use the correct form. Use the hint under the line to help.

| **Word Box** |
| doe, dough |
| to, too, two |
| bore, boar |
| sew, sow |
| whoa, woe |
| hostile, hostel |
| vain, vein |
| toe, tow |
| gait, gate |
| pare, pear, pair |
| counsel, council |
| flour, flower |
| hare, hair |
| fairy, ferry |
| there, their |
| been, bean |
| fair, fare |

1. They didn't have to pay a _____ to cross the river on the _____.
   (token)   (boat)

2. He had _____ asked not to change the date of the _____.
   (past participle of verb)   (exposition)

3. _____ will be _____ extra people at the student
   (pronoun)   (number)
   _____ meeting.
   (assembly)

4. The _____ of the _____ queen
   (tendril(s))   (sorceress)
   was decorated with a _____.
   (blossom)

5. The _____ hopped into the bin to escape a _____ of dogs.
   (animal)   (couple)

6. Using _____ and water he made a _____ to cover the _____ in the pie.
   (meal)   (paste)   (fruit)

7. The _____ conferred with her clients at _____ home.
   (lawyer)   (possessive pronoun)

8. The young man had to _____ a bushel of fruit every day when
   (peel)
   he worked in the kitchen at the _____.
   (inn)

9. The truck will have to _____ the car through the _____.
   (pull)   (door)

10. The rider caught her _____ in the stirrup when the horse changed _____.
    (foot part)   (walk)

11. The young student was so _____ he did not scream when the doctor had to
    (proud)
    _____ up the bleeding _____ in his arm without anesthetic.
    (stitch)   (vessel)

12. "_____, is me. I cannot make peace with my _____ neighbors!"
    (grief)   (unfriendly)

13. The hunter thought he could halt the _____ from charging by calling out _____.
    (wild pig)   (stop)

14. The ground was so dry, she had to _____ a hole in the earth to _____ the _____ plant.
    (drill)   (put in the earth) (seed)

15. The young _____ came _____ the water with her mother to drink, _____.
    (female animal)   (preposition)   (also)

Teacher: The answers to this test are found on page 23.

Name _____   Date _____

Short Answer Test—<u>The Real Thief</u> by William Steig

The questions about *The Real Thief* must be answered in complete sentences. Give as much evidence as possible to support your opinions. You may quote directly from your book. Use the back of the paper if you need more space to write.

1. The job of chief guard bored Gawain. Why had he accepted it? _____

_____

2. Who was Adrian and what did he mean when he said, "Quod erat demonstratum?"

_____

3. If you had been in the courtroom, would you have accepted the king's evidence?

_____

4. Explain why you did or did not accept Basil's judgement. Describe what action you would

have taken to support your opinion. _____

_____

5. Why do you think Derek was sure that he would have confessed if Gawain had been put in

prison? _____

_____

6. Who do you think suffered the most: Derek, Gawain or King Basil? _____

_____

Answers to the questions. 1. Gawain had accepted the boring job because he liked the king very much and would do anything for him. He was like all the other people of the kingdom who held the king in high esteem. 2. Adrian, the cat, held the position of Prime Minister. He said *Quod erat demonstratum* after stating that only Basil and Gawain had the keys to the Treasure. The King would not rob himself, therefore Gawain was the guilty one "which was to be proved." 3. Yes or no in a complete sentence would answer this question. 4. Answers will vary. Must include material from the story to support his or her opinion. 5. Answers will vary. 6. Answers will vary.

MATHEMATICS

Skills

- Tell what the facts are in a given word problem and what needs to be done to solve it.

- Recognize and use mathematical words appropriate to the concept.

- Solve problems that call for one or two operations.

- Choose the appropriate operation(s).

- Write and solve a number sentence that represents a given real-life situation.

- Write a real-life problem that represents a given number sentence.

- Estimate, determine, and interpret the most reasonable solution to a problem.

- Determine if there is too much, too little, or just enough information.

- Make reasonable or logical conjectures and conclusions about situations represented by mathematical sentences using words such as *and, or, if...then, all, some, none, not,* and *out of.*

- Express points, lines, rays, and line segments, and relate them to shapes in the environment.

- Express congruent shapes, line segments, and angles.

- Express properties of the following solids: cone, cube, cylinder, sphere, prism, and pyramid and relate them to shapes in the environment.

- Express properties of parallel, perpendicular, and intersecting lines and relate them to shapes in the environment.

- Express properties of a circle and relate them to shapes in the environment.

- Apply the circumference and area of a circle to shapes in the environment.

- Classify quadrilaterals by shape: square, rectangle, rhombus, parallelogram, and trapezoid.

- Analyze and classify angles: right, acute, and obtuse.

- Classify a triangle by its angles or sides.

- Estimate and verify the perimeter of polygons.

- Estimate and verify the number of plane shapes.

- Estimate and verify the number of degrees in an angle.

- Measure and draw angles.

- Estimate and verify the volume and surface area of solid shapes.

- Estimate and measure length, weight, area, volume, and capacity in customary and metric units.

- Select and use the most appropriate unit to measure length, weight, area, volume, and capacity.

- Read and estimate temperature in Celsius and Fahrenheit.

- Analyze, extend, and create more complex number patterns.

- Analyze and graph an ordered pair for a specific point on a number plane.

- Express additional ordered pairs when discovering a function rule.

- Express the function rule when given ordered pairs.

- Collect, organize, display, interpret, and analyze data in bar, line, and circle graphs, charts, and tables.

- Determine the range, mean, median, and mode from a set of data.

- Predict outcomes and record results of simple probability experiments.

- Use simple tables or tree diagrams to represent possible outcomes of an experiment.

- Express the operation symbol which makes a number sentence true.

- Express the missing number in a number sentence to make a true sentence (commutative, associative, and distributive properties).

- Write a mathematical expression for a phrase or sentence.

- Express a number represented by "n" in an equation.

- Use and explain simple formulas, such as $I = prt$ (Interest= principal x rate x time).

- Analyze and substitute a value for a variable, and simplify.

- Apply number concepts to real problem situations.

- Explore and use the greatest common factor and the least common multiple of a given pair of numbers.

- Investigate prime and composite numbers.

- Analyze the prime factorization of given numbers.

- Develop operation concepts of whole numbers.

- Use a variety of estimation and mental computation strategies when appropriate to find sums, differences, products, or quotients of whole numbers, decimals, or fractions.

- Identify, express, and use the place value of decimals.

- Analyze, compare, order, and round decimals.

- Develop operation concepts of decimals.

- Select and use appropriate method of computing: mental arithmetic, pencil and paper, calculator.

- Explore relationships between fractions and decimals.

- Analyze, compare, and order fractions.

- Analyze and simplify fractions.

- Explore relationship between mixed number and improper fractions.

- Develop operation concepts of fractions and mixed numbers.

- Express the relationship of one number to another as a ratio.

- Analyze and explain methods for solving proportions.

- Identify relationships between percents, fractions, and decimals.

- Explain relationships between whole numbers and integers.

As I wrote in the Overview, much of the year's math curriculum will be review and you'll hear, "We've done that!" or, "We know how to do that." when you ask the students to get out their books to begin answering some questions. It's probably true that they have done work like this before, but not with the same understanding.

> **Things could be worse. Suppose your errors were counted and published every day, like those of a ball player.**
>
> —Anonymous

Math Routines

To begin, decide on a pattern for the week's work: choose a day for the introduction of new material with follow up in class and as homework on a second day, and a third weekday for testing the new concepts, vocabulary and actual process. Fourth day for review of addition or multiplication combinations, you call them out, the students write down only the answers. (You may find that the review of basic facts for computation is not necessary.) The drill work can be checked by a partner, number correct recorded, a retest taken if more than two are wrong. The fifth day can be for workshops, projects, review, and further assessment of the work-to-date.

Averages

Using math in everyday life is probably not something that your students consider seriously. The quote on this page may get them thinking and give you a starting point for the year's work. There is math in things we take for granted. Percentages, graphs, proportions, rates, measurements, and patterns are all part of life's math.

If your school year begins in September, you can start with averages since it's the end of the baseball season and the World Series is about to begin. Many in the class will know the statistics that go with their favorite player on their favorite team: whose batting average was highest, whose pitching best. But do they know how to do the math to arrive at the numbers? And do they know what average means?

Finding averages is a very useful device for putting together all kinds of information and using skills of computation already learned. Begin with information about the class, the school's population and/or the city. Find the average height of all sixth graders (practice measuring), compare with the average height of older students, and also younger students. Record the average temperature for a week, then a month, and find the average. Use the ubiquitous sneaker to provide information to analyze: most popular make, cost, how many does each student own, how often do students have to buy new ones, what other types of shoes do they wear? The list of ideas is endless and the class will probably come up with a number of their own unique ones.

To find significant averages, the information has to have a range or be taken from a large pool. A discussion of the proposed ideas is needed before data is collected and diagnosed. After the information is collected and put into tables, it can be put into graphs. The graph is another way of representing the information visually.

So, through working with averages at the beginning of the year, the class has begun to develop several important skills for looking at information after it has been collected. They have collected data, found averages, made tables, and put their findings into graphs—a combination of thinking, computing, and organizing information to present in graphic form. The final step should be an analysis of individual findings and presentations as well as an evaluation of the work and skill with which it was done.

Evaluation of Math Projects

Evaluation should be based on ease of understanding and the way in which the material is presented. Class members should be included in the evaluation of their own and their classmates' work. Setting up criteria for others can be a way in which a student learns to set standards for him or herself. However, if a student's assessment of his or her own work seems to diverge greatly from yours or the class's evaluation, a private conference with the student should be scheduled.

Algebra Word Problems

Although sixth graders have had experience with "unknowns" and are familiar with the word algebra, they may not have written problems in algebraic form using a letter "x" to stand for the unknown. They have worked out situations that needed a number answer by drawing a diagram, working backward, guessing and checking, or looking for patterns.

This year they need to learn how to put a problem into an algebraic sentence. Most textbooks give them many simple examples to get started: solve for "a" in the following, 9 + a = 16, 6 – a = 2, 28/a = 4, a x 12 = 48. After students have done a number of problems similar to the above example, they should state problem situations in algebraic sentences. Word problems can come from their textbook or "stories" that you have written.

Have students create their own story problems as homework. They should express the story in an equation that represents the way in which it could be solved, and solve the problem. Writing a problem clearly is sometimes as difficult as solving one. The exercise in problem-writing is as valuable as problem-solving since it helps the students express their ideas clearly. Assigning problem-writing as homework with the problem on one page and the equation and solution on another allows for an exchange of questions and answers between students. Combining the student work as a practice sheet for the class adds to the challenge. Having determined that there is enough information given to express in an equation, students should be able to go ahead and solve the problem from the information given. Discussion of different equations written to solve the problems can lead to a discussion of how clearly the original problem was written, and that there can be more than one way to solve a problem.

Equivalent Fractions and Decimals

Fractions are probably the numerical concept that children were first aware of, just as dividing was the first mathematical operation at which they became proficient, even though the solution was arrived at by estimation rather than pencil and paper computation. Splitting goodies so one child has as much as a sibling or friend is something that children start doing before they go to school. But they don't know they've been dividing things up or thinking in terms of parts of a whole, so fractions as numbers, adding and subtracting them or multiplying and dividing them is often difficult. When students see the equivalent value between fractions and decimals they understand better how both sets of numbers express a quantity that is less than a whole. I found that seeing that they are equivalent is helpful in understanding what the different notations mean. Give each student a copy of the equivalent fractions and decimals reference sheet on page 32.

Stock Market Project

To make the relationship between fractions and decimals clearer, assign a project using the stock market. Discuss what the stock market is, what a share is, and how to read the daily quotations. Allow two or three weeks to do the project. Stock quotes can be found in the newspaper or on the Internet. The worksheets for this project are on pages 33 and 34.

Probability

Determining how probability works, and what patterns have to be recorded to figure out the chance of something happening, is the kind of activity that is perfect for small groups at the end of the week. Direct the students to choose partners or divide them up into small groups to work.

Start the discussion by asking if the statements "I bet that you'll get an A," or, "I bet I'll fail," often heard in the classroom, can be proved true or false. How can you decide the outcome of a test? Starting with that idea as an opener, the class can discuss the importance of knowing what is going to happen in science, business, games and elections. Using dice, flips of coins, data about outside events such as a school bus arriving on time, sitting next to someone in class who has blue eyes, are all things that can be looked into, data recorded, and the probability of the outcome determined. Such projects give students opportunities to work together and share their thinking with each other and their findings with the whole class. Have plenty of materials on hand to work with including tables about temperatures, exit polls, and results of elections. Working with probabilities links math with science and social studies.

Recipes for Math

A practical application of computations is increasing recipes. Suggest a class party. Ask students to bring in their favorite recipes with a list of grocery store prices for the ingredients. Based on class size, begin to plan the party with the following questions and stipulations. How many people will attend? Should the recipe be doubled or tripled? Approximate the cost of each dish. Compare the costs of dishes that are similar. Should the choice of which food to serve be based on price alone? What would be a well-balanced supper? Decide the menu, the quantities of food needed, and the other materials you will need such as knives and forks. Write up the menu for the party in an attractive way and have the party! In this project there is a math link with Health and Art.

Other Math Resources

One Grain of Rice by Demi (Scholastic, 1997) is a mathematical folktale about a Raja who thinks he is wise and fair. The book gives students the opportunity to write and read large and larger numbers, explore place value and the power of doubling, mathematically, and as folk wisdom.

The last extra that I suggest is *Donald in Mathmagic Land* (Walt Disney Company, 1998), a wonderful video, starring Donald Duck, in a land of numbers, music and shapes. If your students have studied ancient Greece they will remember something about Pythagoras and his theorem about a right triangle. They may also remember that the Pythagoreans believed that the Earth revolved around a fixed point. It is a wonderful piece to show and can prompt all kinds of investigations, and links Math and Social Studies.

The Desk Project

The desk project is called applied geometry, and also involves skills and talents belonging in Fine Arts. It gives a student the opportunity to create a design in two dimensions and realize it in three. It is an interesting way to experiment with different shapes and see how they function when they are put to practical use. It is also a challenge to draw and build something to scale.

The time frame for this project is two weeks. There are three parts to the assignment and following the steps in sequence is important. Refer to the project sheet on page 35. Students turn designs in to you for approval. Before beginning to design a new desk, the students will have to measure their old ones and decide how this standard for a chair and desk was arrived at. Did the manufacturers seek out the average size of a student? What other information did the builders need before manufacturing the desks in quantity? The project is to be done as homework. Use the approval process to help students organize their time. Invite colleagues to judge the desks when finished.

Table of Equivalents

	Dollar Notation			Decimal	Fraction	Percent
Penny	1	or	.01	.01	1/100	1%
Nickel	5	or	.05	.05	1/20	5%
Dime	10	or	.10	.10	1/10	10%
Quarter	25	or	.25	.25	1/4	25%
Fifty-Cent piece	50	or	.50	.50	1/2	50%
			.75	.75	3/4	75%
Silver Dollar			1.00	1.00	1/1	100%

Decimal and Percent Equivalents of Common Fractions

fraction	decimal	percent
1/8	.125	12.5%
1/6	.166	16.6%
1/4	.25	25%
1/3	.333	33.3%
1/2	.5	50%

To make a fraction into a decimal number, divide the numerator (top number) of the fraction by the denominator (bottom number). The answer is a decimal.

$$\frac{1}{4} : 4\overline{)1.00} \quad = .25 \qquad \frac{1}{3} : 3\overline{)1.00} \quad = .33$$

To make the decimal into a percent number, move the decimal two places to the right. Add the % sign.

$$.25 = 25\% \qquad .33 = 33\%$$

To make a percent into a decimal fraction, drop the % sign, put a line under the number and 100 under the line.

$$19\% = \frac{19}{100} \qquad 75\% = \frac{75}{100}$$

Teacher: Make a copy of this worksheet for each student.

Name _____   Date _____

Be an Investor!

You have $1000 with which to buy a stock that you think may be a good investment. Once you have decided what you want to buy and have found it on either the NY Stock Exchange or NASDAQ listing, determine how many shares you can buy with the money.

Name of Stock _____

Date of Purchase _____

Purchase price of a share as shown in newspaper/Internet _____

Decimal equivalent _____

Number of shares purchased _____

Money left from the $1000 _____

Teacher: Make a copy of this worksheet for each student.

Name of Stock

Date	quote in paper	quote/decimal	Amount of Change +/-	Total cash value

Check your stock at least three times a week, either Monday or Friday and two other days, and fill in this stock sheet. After our tracking period is over, graph the information. You may use graph paper. Be sure that the graph is easy to read and understand.

Teacher: Make a copy of this form for each student.

Name _____   Date _____

The Perfect School Desk

Many different kinds of desks and chairs have been used for studying. Since you have sat in and tried to work at many of them for a number of years, you are an expert in sitting and studying.

Design and build a desk that could be bought for use in our classroom. Consider:

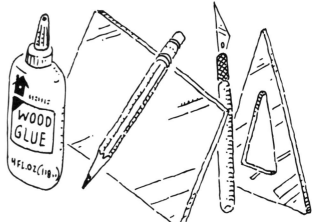

- Size of the room
- Average number of students in the room
- Different activities for which a desk is used
- Materials the desk should be made of
- Whether the desk should be movable

Our class will decide the scale for drawings and model (example 1 inch = 1 foot). _____ You do not have to consider cost even though this is a very important consideration for the school board.

There will be three steps to your design project:

1. Submit a scale drawing of the front and side views with specifications for materials and colors to be used.

   Date due _____ Approved date _____

2. Build a rough model of the design using lightweight cardboard.

   Date due _____ Approved date _____

3. Build a final model. Your final model should use a finer quality cardboard or plastic model board; it should adhere to the scale agreed upon and stand on its own. If you have changed your rough after it had been approved, submit an explanation in writing of why you made the changes when you turn in your final project.

The evaluation of your project will be made on how well you have followed the three steps above. Build the model to scale and put it together so that it will stand on its own. The work must be your own.

Due date: _____

Teacher: Make a copy of this form for each student.

PHYSICAL EDUCATION

Skills

- **Locomotor**—Jump one long and one short rope at the same time for two minutes. Jump "Double Dutch" with jump ropes for two minutes. Jump in rhythm to waltz-time music. Pivot in a basketball game and pass the ball.

- **Manipulative Movements**—Throw a ball for accuracy using a softball throw. Throw a forward pass with accuracy. Throw a lateral pass with accuracy. Catch a softball throw above the waist. Catch a softball throw below the waist. Catch a fly ball. Catch a football throw above the waist. Catch a football throw below the waist. Catch a punted football. Punt a football. Practice place-kicking a football with accuracy. Kick a rolling soccer ball with accuracy. Punt a soccer ball with accuracy. Play a soccer game according to the rules. Trap a soccer ball with a knee trap. Trap a soccer ball with a lower leg trap. Block an attempted soccer goal. Guard an opponent in a basketball game. Shoot a basket from a distance of 5 to 10 feet. Shoot a foul shot from the free-throw line. Dribble a ball below the waist during a basketball game. Play paddle handball. Using a bat, hit a pitched ball with power. Pass the baton during a circular relay.

- **Rhythm and Dance**—Take up correct positions for square dancing. Dance the steps for the Virginia Reel. Perform a two-step. Perform a polka step.

- **Physical Fitness**—Explain the effects on the body of exercise, fatigue, illness, relaxation, and stress. Explain what it means to be physically fit and how to maintain fitness. Design a personal exercise program.

- **Self-Realization**—Set personal goals. Practice skills and new habits on a regular basis to achieve a goal.

- **Group Membership**—Recognize the effort and accomplishments of others. Accept the errors of others without criticism. Participate in dances, team games, sports, and relays.

- **Leadership**—Teach two skills to a small group. Organize and play games when the teacher is not present. Assume different leadership roles at different times. Lead the class in exercises. Demonstrate a new skill or dance step.

- **Recreation**—Develop and improve skills in a wide variety of recreational activities.

Generally the sixth grader goes to Physical Education (PE) because it's fun. "You don't have to learn anything," is a comment you hear. And, it should be fun, but sometimes it's not because the goals require more effort than just fun on the part of the students. The goals of the PE curriculum are twofold. The first is to help a student achieve the body strength that is appropriate to his or her age and physical development. The second is to learn to play a number of team sports that help develop cooperative play and the coordination to catch throw or kick a ball. Both goals are directly connected to the health of an individual though the curriculum is not directly tied to that of Health.

> The play of shine and shade on the trees as the supple boughs wag,
>
> The delight alone or in the rush of the streets, or along the fields and hill-sides,
>
> The feeling of health, the full-noon trill, the song of me rising from bed and meeting the sun.
>
> —Walt Whitman, "Song of Myself"

Fitness

The fitness part of the program is made up of a series of exercises to increase strength, endurance, and flexibility. The exercise routine may be a full 45-minute period once or twice a week or be part of each scheduled PE period with five minutes of stretches and ten of exercises before other activities begin. Some record should track the progress of each student. Since wellness and a consciousness of one's physical fitness has become an important part of our culture, it is appropriate that these routines be taught in school and emphasis put on the health benefits of exercising. Doing a routine two, three, or more times a week may help young people become aware of the benefits of exercise as being as important to health as eating well and having sufficient rest each night. Use a period that has been set aside for the health curriculum to discuss the benefits of fitness including the importance of diet and rest.

Separate Gym Periods

Sixth-grade students are in transition from child to teen and their bodies are undergoing the stress of change. Each student needs to be aware of his or her own body and its particular needs. Because the changes the students are experiencing have to do with their sexuality and foster self-consciousness, many schools separate the girls and boys for gym class.

Gym Period

First the class warms up with exercising or a quick jog around the field or the gym. Then the class concentrates on developing a particular skill such as passing and receiving a ball either by kicking or throwing it and taking the ball down the court to score a goal. After practicing dribbling or taking the ball down the field with small kicks, students divide up and half of them start playing interference. The practice helps strengthen large muscles in arms and legs as well as being cardio-respiratory exercise. Keep students moving energetically so that they develop their muscles and a specific skill in game playing.

Sixth-grade students are old enough to ready themselves for high school competition games, so team sports make up much of the gym period. Teams representing the school are formed. Often a sixth grader will be part of that team. Games played vary depending on the part of the country you are in. Depending on the size of the school, the team play can be intramural as well as intermural. Often, for both girls and boys, team sports practice takes place after school rather than during the gym period.

The head of the PE department and gym teacher or coach, as well as the homeroom teacher, all have the responsibility of teaching and encouraging sportsmanship among teammates and toward the opposing team. Being able to accept losses as well as victories, fouls, and injuries are all part of the game.

SCIENCE

Skills

- Identify and delineate problems by questioning which may be answered through investigation.

- Design experiments with controls and variables to support or refute a hypothesis.

- Predict and draw inferences from data.

- Ask relevant questions and describe expected outcomes from past data.

- Generate data by investigation, quantitative measurement, and reference reading.

- Explore, observe, and examine objects to collect and interpret data.

- Identify, name, and measure the conditions of changing events and materials.

- Record, organize, and communicate procedures and data in oral and written form.

- Recognize the differences between facts and hypotheses.

- Identify statements or quantitative data from investigations which have a direct relationship to the solution of a problem.

- Recall information formerly obtained and integrate it with new information.

- Determine the need to repeat observations as a means of verifying data.

- Follow directions and safety procedures when investigating and handling chemicals, science equipment, and animals.

- Utilize reading and language skills in comprehending science content by using textbooks and reference and media materials.

- Use mathematical books in solving problems.

- Develop a science vocabulary.

> **Be true to your teeth, then they'll never be false to you.**
>
> —Soupy Sales

HEALTH

Skills

- Recognize that a lifelong relationship exists between health care habits and well-being. Identify behaviors to reduce risks of cardiovascular disorders such as the lack of exercise, being overweight, and a diet high in sugars and fats.

- Analyze the physical, emotional, and social changes which occur during puberty and recognize that it starts at different times for different people. Understand that the male and female have a role in human reproduction and responsible parenting, and that sexual behavior is a personal decision and one must be responsible. Predict that the outcome of sexual behavior may be pregnancy and/or disease. Describe ways to be assertive in dealing with sexual pressures. Please note, in many schools and districts this section of the health curriculum requires parental consent.

- Describe the effects of food on performance and behavior. Compare and contrast the cost of various foods to their nutritional values. Relate functions of food nutrients in meeting body needs for persons of different ages, genders, sizes, and activity levels. Identify concept of energy balance in relation to the amounts of food eaten. Analyze essential components of a balanced diet for age-group. Modify food selections to increase consumption of a variety of high-fiber foods such as fresh fruits, vegetables, and whole grains products while reducing consumption of sweets, fats, and fried or salty foods.

- Analyze factors that contribute to self-worth. Recognize and respect the worth and contributions of others. Develop caring relationships with family and friends. Identify the effects of stress and manage stress appropriately. Analyze ways to reduce and control feelings of anger. Apply processes of problem solving to conflict resolution. Analyze the influences of peer pressure on choices and behavior. Identify ways to be assertive, especially in dealing with peer pressure. Accept responsibility for own actions.

- Consider consequences that may result from using or choosing not to use substances. Recognize that individual decisions are influenced by a variety of pressures. Identify and apply effective ways to resist pressures to use substances. Examine reasons why people choose to use or choose not to use substances. Participate in activities that promote healthy alternatives to substance abuse.

- Classify environmental factors that may cause diseases and disorders. Distinguish those diseases caused by microorganisms from diseases resulting from other factors. Discuss natural and acquired body defenses against disease. Identify ways infectious diseases are spread, including HIV/AIDS.

- Enumerate the benefits of health care. Explore ways community health problems can be prevented or solved by the cooperation of workers from various agencies. Incorporate recycling into one's lifestyle. Identify threats to a healthy and safe environment.

- Differentiate between good and bad touching. List steps taken if someone touches a person in a way that makes him or her feel uncomfortable. Analyze precautions for self-protection in public places. Recognize the difference between nurturing, confusing, and exploitative touches. Know what constitutes an emergency and whom to call for help. Recognize the symptoms of choking, and learn the Heimlich maneuver.

Schools with a Science Specialist

During the years that I taught sixth grade I was most fortunate to work in a school where there was a science specialist. The subject did not have to be included in parts of my curriculum. However, I was in close contact with the teachers of the science program so I knew what my class was studying and was aware when there were opportunities to support and enrich science concepts in my areas of the curriculum. The metric system (Math), historical figures who had investigated some of the concepts students were studying (Social Studies), and biographies of scientific innovators (Literature) were three points of possible connection. If you are in a school system that has a science specialist and a lab, then you will be responsible for making connections between your areas of teaching and the science curriculum.

Precambrian Time

Almost 4 billion years ago
beginning 4.5 billion (?)

Paleozoic Era

Cambrian Period
70 million years (?)
began 570 million

Ordovician Period
65 million years
began 500 million

Siurian Period
25 million years
began 435 million

Devonian Period
50 million years
began 410 million

Carboniferous Period

Mississippian Period
30 million years

Pennsylvanian Period
40 million years
began 360 million

Permian Period
50 million years
began 290 million

Mesozoic Era

Triassic Period
35 million years
began 240 million

Jurassic Period
67 million years
began 205 million

Cretaceous Period
75 million years
began 138 million

> **The whole of science is nothing more than a refinement of everyday thinking.**
>
> —Albert Einstein, "Physics and Reality," 1936

Teamwork in the Content Areas

Math, Social Studies, Science and Language Arts are big content areas. If there are several sixth grades, you may be able to arrange with a colleague to teach one of the content areas to the classes, while you teach another to the same classes in exchange.

Student Organization in Science

The standards and expectations for studying, using the correct materials, keeping homework up-to-date, and finishing assignments neatly and in a timely manner also apply to the study of science. If the class uses a lab, review the safety rules and procedures to follow in that classroom. Organizing the information that is given in the text, discussions, handouts and videos is an important challenge for the year and throughout the students' school experiences. You must help your disorganized students with the organizational process, including learning how to take notes, outlining, and organizing information.

Each division of study in science has its vocabulary. Students should keep a glossary of new science words in their notes—perhaps in a special section of their notebooks. You might have word lists ready with space where students write the definitions they have looked up.

Science Activities

Science in sixth grade begins the ordering of knowledge. Looking at information and putting it into categories is a very important tool to further learning of all kinds.

The origin of the sun, the Earth and the beginning of life on this planet are the basis for the year's study. Discussion of students' ideas about what life or a living thing is and what an organism needs to exist leads to generalizations that can be used to make a list of the characteristics of living things. Birth, growth, difference in size, needing air, light and food are all ideas that may be given. Taking what has been volunteered in the discussion, direct their thinking to an awareness of the fact that whatever the size of the living organism, it is made up of small units or cells. These first living units began forming three and a half billion years ago. The Earth itself is older.

Geologic Time Line of the Earth

The age of the earth and when life appeared on this planet can be shown on a time line. Rolls of two-inch wide paper tape (adding machine tape) are wonderful for this project. Using the scale of a meter equals one billion years (1 m = 1 billion years), several meters of paper will be unrolled before people appear on the line. On their own or with a partner, students can make timelines using the scale above, including as much information as possible such as the names and dates of the geologic eras—Cenozoic, Mesozoic, Paleozoic, and Precambrian, and the periods and epochs within those eras. When plants and different animals appeared within specific time frames would also be appropriate entries on the timelines. Some students might include a great deal of detail with pictures or drawings of different life forms showing when they emerged. Students might develop a different format to expand the project to include more detailed information.

Earth on a 24-hour Clock

Another way to highlight what happened over the millennia is to divide a clock into 24-hour sections. In a picture that the eye takes in at one glance, people's appearance on this planet just seconds before 24:00 PM makes a very strong visual statement about human life on earth. Assigning timelines to show the history of the Earth helps to make time graphically comprehensible. Students see how short the time span is that Homo sapiens has existed on this planet. Using the time frame that some scientists present, it is important to remind students that there are many theories about when and how life began.

Cenozoic Era

Tertiary Period

Paleocene Epoch
8 million years
began 63 million

Eocene Epoch
17 million years
began 55 million

Oligocene Epoch
14 million years
began 38 million

Miocene Epoch
19 million years
began 24 million

Pliocene Epoch
3 million years
began 5 million

Quaternary Period

Pleistocene Epoch
2 million years
began 2 million

Holocene Epoch
10,000 years
began 10,000 years

Geologic Time Line

24 hours = 4.5 billion years

1 hour (from 1-2 on clock) = 187,500,000 years

1 minute (1/60 space from 1-2) = 3,108,333 years

1 second (1/3,600 of space from 1-2) = 51,805 years

Human beings have been on earth almost 39 seconds on this clock

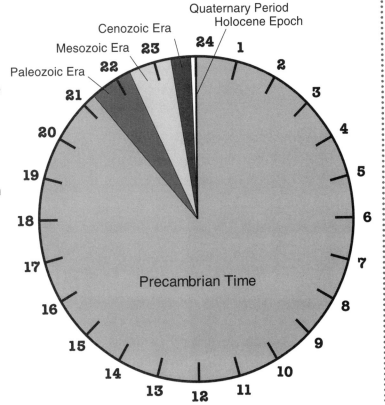

41

List of scientific terms for study of single cell structure

prokaryotic cells

eukaryotic cells

organelles & other cell parts

cell membrane

cell membrane transport

photosynthesis

cellular respiration

asexual reproduction

mitosis

sexual reproduction

meiosis

genes

genetics

laws of inheritance

chromosomes

DNA

molecule

protein synthesis

mutations

Single Cell Structure

Study the structure of a cell. How does this organism gets what it needs to live, and what supplies it with energy or food? Through discussion, the students can see that the sun is the important source of energy for all life. How this energy is absorbed and used by the cell leads to studying cell structure: the two basic types of cells, their parts, how they move, eat, breathe, and reproduce. Studying single cell structure and labeling its parts gives the students knowledge of the basic life form that multiplies to create multi-celled beings in both the plant and animal worlds. The study of cells begins the process of sorting and putting into categories what scientists have learned about our world. And the study of the cell generates a scientific vocabulary that will be used in classes in high school and college.

Tip

Have plenty of workspace and equipment available so everyone can participate.

Human Reproduction

Since all life shares the characteristic of reproduction and growth, human reproduction is part of the science curriculum. In many schools and districts this is a curriculum item which needs special parental consent before students can receive instruction. However, because the sixth-grade students are experiencing the changes in their bodies that will enable them to reproduce, the discussion of this aspect of Life Science is also a part of the Health curriculum.

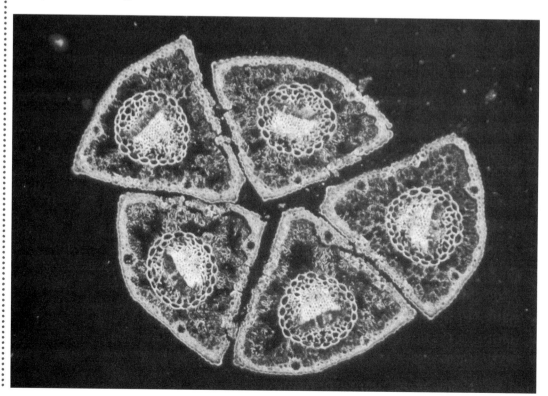

For this part of the curriculum, male and female students are separated to view films or videos that show the growth, change, and function of the reproductive organs. By sixth grade many of the students may have seen these films several times. Often they are acquainted not only with the films, but with the changes as well because they have experienced them in their own bodies. Most of the girls will have started their menstrual cycle and some of the boys will have experienced nocturnal emissions. Much of the discussion is more productive when it is carried on in a single sex group with a nurse or other adult figure who can answer technical biological questions.

The Emotional Side of the Science of Human Reproduction

Because the physical changes have emotional repercussions, have the whole class get together after the biological information has been presented.

Below you will find a quote that is good advice to a sixth grader who is struggling with what and who he or she is.

Students at this age are often super-sensitive about appearances. Some will react to negative comments about how they look by lashing out at their friends with equally nasty comments. Others will retreat into themselves, feeling awful about a comment, even one said in fun. Being sensitive to the reactions of others is a very important part of the emotional well-being of the group and should be talked about. Depending on your personality, you may wish to have this discussion with your class or have another teacher come to share the discussion about feelings with your class, while you go to his or hers. You may prefer to discuss these matters with a group you don't see as often. On the other hand, it may be better to have

discussions of feelings among a small group of students in the class. The sessions involving feelings should help students in their interactions in the school community. The sessions are important and should be handled thoughtfully. If you have an extremely sensitive or angry student in your class, you may feel that a call home to arrange for a conference between you and the student's parents would be helpful. However, if you suspect that the student has more serious problems than those of the average sixth grader, your administration should be advised and they can make the decision as to whom to consult.

Depending on your school's calendar, these aspects of the health curriculum may be scheduled at a particular time of the year, they may be ongoing (once a month or week), or they may be left to your discretion. However the health issues are dealt with in the curriculum, you should be ready to discuss an issue that seems to trouble a student whether it has to do with personal or biological issues.

> **Do not wish to be anything but what you are, and try to be that perfectly.**
>
> **—unknown**

43

Heredity

One of the most interesting things in the study of life science is heredity—why you have the color eyes you have, the color hair you have, your body frame, and so on. My colleague, Steven Schwartz, designed a project to help students supplement their textbook information about heredity by observing and recording. The worksheets on pages 46–48 support this project.

Begin with the worksheet titled *Which Human Alleles Are Dominant?* (page 46) Explain that alleles are one or two alternative forms of a gene occupying the same chromosome. As an introduction to heredity, collect data from the class about these easily identifiable genetic traits. Have students fill in the chart provided on the worksheet with the raw data, and analyze results to determine which alleles are dominant.

Once they have completed this introductory research, they are ready to work on the lab project using the worksheets on pages 47 and 48. Using the drawing of *Labicus animalis* as a reference, have students prepare a drawing of each parent. Mother and father are both whiskered, black-eyed, brown-furred, with straight tails and pointed ears. The parents are heterozygous, which means they carry the genes for both traits except sex.

Science Fair

Many schools require a major science independent-research project on a subject chosen by the student to be exhibited and defended at a Science Fair. At my school, the student chooses a topic, and hypothesizes about the results of certain testing conditions over a period of time. The hypothesis is tested by experimental conditions the student devises to test the proposed idea. All findings were written up and displayed with illustrations and text.

Everyone's work is exhibited at the annual Science Fair. All the students stand or sit at their displays to explain and defend their work.

Wisdom is meaningless until your own experience has given it meaning.

—Bergen Evan

Outside Resources

Since the school where I worked is in New York City, Mr. Schwartz took the class to the Museum of Natural History to see the exhibit of bio-diversity. The museum also has exhibitions relevant to the study of cells and a trip to one of those exhibitions was planned during the year. Using outside sources like these is a wonderful way to expand the learning arena. Often the photo illustrations in textbooks are photos of exhibits in museums. Using such exhibitions affords you a wonderful opportunity to share with your students. You can make up study-sheets to hand out at the beginning of your visit. This will enable the students to look at dioramas or models with a more critical eye. It is a very different kind of trip than the trip your students make with their families.

A one day or an overnight trip to a campsite where students can explore a natural environment may be planned as part of the science curriculum and also be an interesting adventure in group dynamics. Getting information about organizations that sponsor such experiences in your area is worthwhile. *Nature's Classroom* is the name of a group that we used for a number of years. Over the course of three to five days the teachers in *Nature's Classroom* introduced students to a variety of experiences involving most of the disciplines studied in school during the middle years. The program also stressed using cooperation to solve difficult problems and a study of environmental issues. Find more information about Nature's Classroom at http://www.naturesclassroom.com. Contact local representatives of the National Park Service, or State and County Parks for information about programs they may offer.

A learning activity used to study the skies is a STARLAB portable planetarium. It is a plastic dome that is inflated with an air pump and seats, at least 20 students. Constellations of the Northern Hemisphere, with figures of the mythic Greek gods drawn around the star groups, is one program that can be projected. Another is the same sky with drawings around the stars that represent the legendary figures of Native American

peoples. It affords the city dweller a wonderful view of the night sky with groups of constellations clearly highlighted. Viewing the constellations connects the literature in legends of the ancient Greeks and other cultures to the study of the sky and science. STARLAB information can be obtained from,

Learning Technologies, Inc.
40 Cameron Ave.
Sumerville, Mass. 02144.
Telephone 1-800/537-8703
http://www.starlab.com

On the website LTI also provides information about how to fund the purchase of a portable planetarium.

Helpful Organizations

There are many organizations that can answer questions you have about a particular aspect of the science curriculum. One of the most helpful organizations is the National Science Teachers Association. Membership gets you a monthly magazine with information and useful lesson plans. My colleague, Mr. Schwartz's use of the cards in the heredity investigation was a modification and refocusing of a lesson plan in the magazine. The lesson plans are all hands-on. Each month they also feature some special article in the magazine about a science issue. Their website is http://www.nsta.org.

Directing questions to NASA will result in materials for your class. For the sixth-grade study of stars and galaxies the science department obtained a Learning EdVenture on planets from Challenger Center for Space Science Education. The kit included work sheets for the students and teacher notes. Much of this information from NASA is available on the World Wide Web at http://www.nasa.gov.

Name _____   Date _____

Which Human Alleles are Dominant?

	Number of Students	Percentage of Students	Appears to be dominant or recessive?	Symbol	Possible Genotype
PTC Taster					
Tongue Roller					
Attached Earlobes					
Blue Eyes					
Dimples					
Short Index Finger					
Hitch-Hiker's Thumb					
Widow's Peak					

PTC taster—Using the chemical Phenylchiocarbamide will help determine the presence of the dominant gene. Subject will detect a bitter taste if the gene is present. PTC can be found at a science supplier.

Tongue Roller—A tongue roller can curl up the sides of the tongue.

Blue eyes is a recessive trait.

Short Index Finger—To determine a "short index finger," the pointer, or index finger, is compared to the length of the fourth (ring) finger.

LAB: Inheritance of Multiple Characteristics

Organism: Labicus animalis
Chromosome Number: 12

(6 pairs)

CHARACTERISTIC	GENOTYPE	PHENOTYPE	GENOTYPE	PHENOTYPE
whiskers	NN Nn	WHISKERED	nn	no whiskers
eyes	EE Ee	BLACK EYES	ee	red eyes
ears	RR Rr	POINTED EARS	rr	rounded ears
tail	TT Tt	STRAIGHT TAIL	tt	curly tail
fur	FF Ff	BROWN FUR	ff	white fur
gender	XX	FEMALE	XY	male

1. Cut each of six index cards into four equally sized pieces. (total—24).

2. Prepare four cards for each trait. On one side label the characteristic (e.g., EYES), and on the reverse side write the allele (e.g., E or e).

   Prepare four cards: Two for the dominant allele (E,E)

   Two for the recessive allele (e,e)

   Make three X cards and 1 Y card for sex.

3. Arrange your cards so that you can cross a male and a female Labicus animalis, both of which are heterozygous for all traits except sex.

4. Place the cards into a metal can, shake, and randomly draw cards until you have two for each of the six traits.

5. Write the genotypes in the spaces provided and complete the drawing of your "animal." on the worksheet *Lab: Transmissions of Genetic Characters in Lab Animal* (page 48)

GENOTYPE _____

_____

_____

_____

_____

Phenotype

GENDER: _____

SOCIAL STUDIES

Skill

- Written sources of information related to certain topics include books, newspapers, magazines, dictionaries, documents, ledgers, encyclopedias, bibliographies, and atlases. Information can also be acquired from radio, television, computer software, the Internet, film, video, and from other people.

- Listen to receive directions and explanations, to expand word meaning, to comprehend ideas, to identify a problem, to determine the point of view of a speaker, and to interpret and evaluate ideas.

- Use the following parts of a book to find information: title page, table of contents, chapter/unit headings, index, and glossary.

- Collect and use information on a selected topic, write an explanation using the facts.

- Compare information selected from various sources.

- Discriminate between primary and secondary source materials.

- Arrange or structure information to facilitate many learning experiences.

- Answer questions related to a unit of study, orally, and in writing.

- Prepare oral and written communications about a variety of topics including descriptions of people, objects, events, and feelings; including news articles for a school newspaper expressing a point of view.

- Organize information to create plays, puppet shows, original classroom dances, songs, and instrumental renditions, and prepare materials for and take part in debates and discussion.

- Take notes and arrange them for a specific purpose.

- Prepare and use simple outlines to organize writing and research.

- Prepare simple bibliographies.

- Identify various physical and human-made features such as land masses, bodies of water, and bridges illustrated on a map.

- Recognize and apply map and globe concepts and terms such as compass, direction, latitude, longitude, the International Date Line, and solar system.

- Identify, describe, read, and use map compass, scales, and grid maps.

- Compare, identify, describe, and read various types of maps including resources and products, vegetation, population, transportation, climate, and historical.

- Relate how climate and the Earth's physical features have factored into the culture of an area.

49

- Recognize the relationship of political boundaries to conflicts among nations.

- Compute distances between points using a mileage scale.

- Interpret, prepare, and explain graphic materials such as charts, pictures, tables, time lines, cartoons, posters, and graphs.

- Interpret pictures by relating pictorial content to main ideas and supporting details.

- Categorize and classify information.

- Place chronological facts and events in sequential order.

- Analyze and compare information contained in various graphic materials.

- Create individual posters and cartoons to express particular ideas.

- Compare ideas contained in various sources by identifying similarities and differences among the ideas.

- Explain main and supporting ideas in pictures, stories, and paragraphs.

- Differentiate between fact and opinion or relevant and irrelevant information.

- Synthesize known information by combining ideas in a different and original way.

- Express opinions based on appropriate information. Use logic in addressing issues.

- Use correct terminology in explaining or discussing information.

- Demonstrate conceptual understanding about a topic under study.

- Use given facts about a society to formulate hypotheses and reach conclusions about the past or the present.

- Reserve judgment until opposing sides in a controversy have been heard.

- Judge the merits of an issue; make choices based on possible consequences to individuals and society.

- Identify and analyze problems or issues.

- Formulate possible solutions to the problems or issues.

- Develop a course of action.

- Evaluate the solution and draw conclusions.

- Identify ways in which resolving value conflicts may change behavior.

- Identify or state examples of value conflicts related to school.

- Identify the following values when presented in actions or words: integrity, courage, reverence, responsibility, justice, love, respect, and law and order.

- Clarify personal values.

- Cooperate with others on projects.

- Assist others who are working to achieve a common goal.

> To regard teachers—in our entire educational system, from the primary grades to the university—as priests of our democracy is therefore not to indulge in hyperbole. It is the special task of teachers to foster those habits of open-mindedness and critical inquiry which alone make for responsible citizens, who, in turn, make possible an enlightened and effective public opinion.
>
> —Felix Frankfurter, opinion, Wieman v. Updegraff, 1952

Social studies, history, is my favorite part of the curriculum. In it you tie together all the skills that you teach, and use writing, reading, science, and math to learn about the particular period of time that your state or school system specifies. My classes studied the Middle Ages and the Renaissance, a wonderfully colorful era with opportunities for use of the fine arts to reinforce the academics. Your school or district may want you to concentrate on the Ancient Civilizations—prehistoric peoples, Mesopotamia, Ancient Egypt, Ancient India, Ancient China, the Ancient Israelites, The Ancient Greeks, Classical Greece, and the rise and fall of the Roman Empire.

The choice of theme or subject for the curriculum should provide opportunities for the student to understand how environment, social and geographic, has influenced the development of cultures in the past and what will happen in the future. Much of history is a reflection of events that have occurred among people brought together in unity or disunity to share the necessities of life. Studying the past should also help students see that the speed and ease with which people can now travel from place to place, plus almost instant communication between people about events that occur has made the planet a more familiar place. There are few unexplored areas or dark ages.

As in science, the time line is an exciting tool for visualizing information. Imagine how the time lines that your students have created during their school careers have changed; from picturing their own lives on a line to picturing eras of billions of years, periods of millions of years, and epochs of thousands of years using a similar line.

Though studying European history may seem Euro-Caucasian chauvinistic, it can be made inclusive by exploring cultures that coexisted in Asia and Africa during the same time periods. Another reason to look at European history is that English is the primary language of this country. English contains many words that come from different European roots. These are things that teachers need to consider when planning for the year. It is important to have a rationale for

including and excluding a nation, a culture, or a race in our study of the past and present.

Geography

Start the year with geography. Ask random questions about what the difference is between political and physical geography. give a quick test to locate important areas on the globe, including your town or city, major bodies of water, some countries (use countries that students in your class have emigrated from or have relatives in), and important urban centers such as London, Beijing, Moscow, Washington, D.C., Buenos Aires, Tokyo, Cairo, Karachi, Delhi, Jerusalem, Baghdad, Sarajevo, and other areas playing a part in world events. History is the story or prelude to what is happening today.

Spend a week introducing the physical geography of the Earth and discuss how the forces of nature—weather, seismic activity, movement of tectonic plates, and astronomical events—have changed it. Explore how three dimensions are pictured on maps using longitude, latitude, scale, and symbols to represent the surface of the earth in two dimensions. Discuss why different kinds of projections were devised to picture areas on the globe and which type of map projection is best for what purpose. Assume that this study is review and, with the exception of political designations that often change, a week should be enough time to cover the material. If it is evident to you that the material is new to your students, you will have to adjust your lesson plans to include teaching this information.

During the second week have each student highlight a geographic area that the class will be studying historically. What is this area like now? Has it changed significantly? Any region that has gone from an agricultural culture and economy to an industrial one, more or less successfully, will have changed significantly. What the changes are and how they occurred will be the subject of the class. This is a very broad outline that can be made to fit most curricular models.

Mapping

Have each student map the area to be studied. Include physical features like rivers, mountains, and large bodies of water. Because my class studied Europe during the 11th- through 16th-centuries my students included information about natural vegetation. I required students to use an atlas that showed the natural vegetation of Europe during that time as a reference map. Political boundaries and cities would not be included. Such a map sets the stage for the events that are to happen.

Social Studies Projects

Because I think that sixth graders learn most effectively by doing projects I'll describe some that I used that can be modified to fit other subject matter.

Set the Stage

First, for all projects, set the stage. Have students make a map and read in any text materials about events that may have taken place over a period of several hundred years.

Make a Tapestry

I base this project on the Bayeux Tapestry made in 1066 A.D by a group of women in Normandy (now in France) to mark the important historical events of the time—the Norman invasion of what is now England and the appearance of Halley's Comet. I took this work of embroidery as the model for the project. We did not have a reproduction of the work, but from small pictures in our text and other sources the idea of what the artisans did was vivid. The women of Bayeux created the story in drawings using wool on linen, and identified leading characters by embroidering their names and words describing what they had done boldly in Latin. As a historical document, it recreated the preparations for the battle and showed how the soldiers were dressed and armed.

The students worked individually, but the pieces that each made went together to tell a story. The class went back in time to the beginning of the seventh century. People in Europe whose land and government had been unified by the Roman Empire were suffering from the chaos created by the lack of this strong force. Slowly groups of powerful lords spread their rule over territories in Western Europe and kingdoms formed. In the 11th-century when King Edward died without an heir, William the Conqueror invaded the island and established Norman rule.

Developing Background

The class did not copy what had already been done so well. In the style of the tapestry, students depicted important characters that we had studied. I gave the students a list of important names from which to choose the one that they wanted to depict. Once they had chosen the person they would draw, they did some research about him or her. The portraits were done as full figures and some symbol of their work or interest showed in the background. The papers were all the same size and a ground line served to connect them. The students all knew that they were limited to the eight colors used in the tapestries. These were colors from plants that had dyed the wool thread used to embroider the linen. The class also looked at other works of art of the period to give them more ideas about the way in which figures were represented at that time. The added information that was needed to complete the project enriched the learning about the Middle Ages. When all the pieces were put together, the final work had a unity and quality of medieval times. Though the preliminary sketches and discussion of what had to be done took place in the classroom, the actual painting was finished in the art studio with the cooperation of the art teacher.

Although each student could have made his or her own drawing/cartoon strip of some event in the history that we had covered, there was a grandness to the project that came about as a result of everyone having had a hand in the final long painting. Being given specific boundaries in color and style the work of the students who had more trouble drawing, could still fit into the whole. There was clarity to the design and a unity of style reflecting the artistic work of the period. The class enjoyed seeing it displayed outside the classroom.

You could use a similar production process to recreate the murals inside an Egyptian tomb (draw with pastels instead of markers to give a sense of dusty age), the Gates of Ishtar in Babylon, an ancient Greek temple as originally painted, or the temple paintings of the ancient Mayas or Aztecs in the Americas.

> The condition of the true artisan, perhaps, is most nearly akin to the gifted schoolteacher's: an all but anonymous calling that allows for mastery, even for a sort of genius, but rarely for fame, applause, or wealth, whose chief reward must be the mere superlative doing of the thing.
>
> —John Barth, "Teacher: The Making of a Good One," Harper's, 1986

Homework

Readings in the textbook were assigned as homework. Usually the reading would be discussed the following day with questions about fact, vocabulary, and opinions as to whether the action was wise or fair.

"Pop" Quizzes

Sometimes I would give a "pop" quiz that included a few questions to check to see if the reading had been done and if my expectations of the level of understanding were sound. In the beginning I would tell students when I made the assignment that I might give a "pop" quiz. I mentioned the possibility a few times when making assignments to impress them with the fact that they were responsible for doing the reading homework. To encourage note-taking, I allowed students to use their notes for the quizzes. This helped to teach techniques of outlining and note taking. As the year went on students would ask if I were going to give a quiz and I would answer that it wouldn't be a "pop quiz" if I told them. They caught on and were usually prepared. I also encouraged them to use the quizzes to help prepare for tests that covered several chapters.

Discussion Points

Using the story of the invasion of England in 1066 as an example there was much to discuss. Who was the rightful heir to the throne after King Edward's death? Should it have been the King's nephew's son Edgar, Harold Godwin appointed by the King's council, Norway's Harald Hardrada, or William of Normandy? Since each man had a just claim, the discussion in the classroom could become lively and, with encouragement lead to a scene in a courtroom that could be prepared for the next class.

Not all events are as dramatic as the Norman invasion of England. Questions could do with everyday concerns of living. How did the people keep warm, what did they eat, was there any entertainment, what kind of life did you live if you weren't a king or pharaoh, or high priest? Have students develop discussion questions about the issues and events they study.

Historical Fiction

Since the textbook is written to give facts and their outcomes, using historical novels helped enrich the history of an era. I included many titles of really wonderful stories, which have a sound historic basis, in my trade book list on pages 19 and 20. I assigned some of the titles to be read as seriously as sections in the textbook. The trade books give a dimension to historic figures that most textbooks don't include. The fictional characters portrayed, usually the age of students in the class, help to make the everyday life of the period interesting and easy to identify with. They also serve as inspirations or models when I ask the class to improvise scenes based on historical happenings.

> **Imagination is more important than knowledge.**
>
> —**Albert Einstein, On Science**

Using Improvisational Theater

I feel putting learning into dramatic form works very well with this age. However, I prefer the scenes be the result of improvisation rather than lines learned from a script, because students are freer to be their chosen character when they do not have to worry about remembering lines. Each student in the play is in command of what he or she has to say. Costumes and very simple props and set complete the play. Everyone in the class has to be an actor, a costumer, set designer and prop person. In other words, the student-actor becomes a person of that time. The students are responsible for the way they appear in the scene and what surrounds them.

Prepare for a improvisation in advance. Introduce the idea and practice role-playing in the class, by first presenting students with a specific situation for characters they will assume. Have them react to an event "in character," and explain their choices of reaction. Gradually expand the time frame of the role-play, and add student "character" interactions. When the students feel comfortable with the concept, tell them that you will be doing an improvisational play as a class.

Each year's class came up with its own ideas of what to do and how to put it together. Some classes needed more prompting than others, but the work always resulted in bringing to life what had been important to the students in the curriculum. They were never big productions but were enjoyed by the classes on our floor. I felt the process of putting the scenes together was the important learning—the history they researched and the interacting with their peers.

The scenes varied from year to year but often there is a fair or action in an inn. One year there was a quarrel at the inn between the innkeeper and a merchant who had come to stay but thought the fee for keeping his horse in the stable was too high. Minstrels were sleeping at the inn also and when the argument was settled they played for all the people having their suppers around the fireplace. We had two recorder players and a violinist. Another year students recreated a fair and a student who could juggle entertained everyone who had come to the performance. Sometimes students recreated jousts on horseback and swordplay. Once the Adam and Eve story was retold with a student taking the role of the snake. Such stories were often presented at medieval fairs to tell people the stories in the Bible, because much of the population could not read. One year several students reenacted the death of the Archbishop of Canterbury. It was very dramatic. Another time the music teacher taught a group a stick dance accompanied by several recorder players from the class.

Another goal that I had as a teacher of Social Studies was to help the students understand that even though the events were long ago they had parallels in today's world. William the Conqueror wanted to know what he ruled and started what could be though of as the first census, the *Domesday Book*. The battles between kings and the church for power, between religions for a people's allegiance, struggle between the elite and the common person for the use of land are all conflicts that continue today.

New technology such as the longbow, introduction of gunpowder, invention of movable type, technique of paper making, all changed the pace of life. Technology in the modern age has done the same only the pace of change is even faster. Other events such as The Black Plague which reduced the population of Europe by almost three-quarters, the signing of the Magna Carta reducing the absolute power of a monarch, and the division of the Catholic Church made great differences in the organization of the world at that time. How the changes affected the people then are the ideas important for the students to think about. Using a time line helps students see how events related to each other and also how these important events and discoveries were the impetus for other things happening.

Symposia

An extension of our improvisational theater was our group discussions. We would choose an issue from the historical period we were studying, choose representative historical personages, research their points of view, and discuss the various facets of the issue as a group. This forum can also be used to discuss modern-day problems. We would move chairs into a circle, or put several together to form Roman-style couches that students could lounge on to help create the mood.

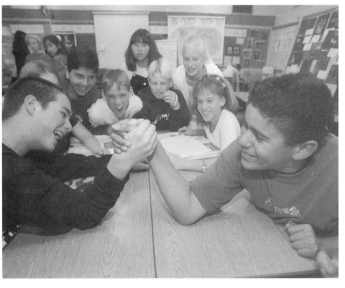

Style Sheet

Bibliography

Metzo, Kiriki de Diego, *Getting Ready to Teach Sixth Grade*, Torrance, Frank Schaffer Publications, Inc., 1999

Footnote

[1]Kiriki de Diego Metzo, *Getting Ready to Teach Sixth Grade*, p. 56.

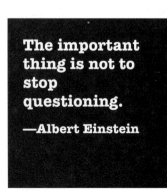

The important thing is not to stop questioning.

—Albert Einstein

Social Studies Research Project

Assign a term paper based on research about a topic or a biography. Discuss your plans with the school librarian before making the assignment. The librarian may have suggestions for topics based on the strength of the library collection, and will be prepared for student questions. Outline your expectations and define work standards to students. Review rules for correctly annotating sources. For the first written project, require that at least two different encyclopedias be used plus another reference book, which would usually be one that deals very specifically with the topic. It could be an autobiography or biography of the person who has been chosen, another history book, or a book that deals with some aspect of life during the correct period of time.

Hand out a style sheet for the bibliography and footnotes and remind students to use them.

Have students decide on a topic. Students outline the kind of information to be included in the report. Architecture, clothing, the art of painting and music, food, chivalry or other rules of manners, education, the structure of society, law, and justice are all possible subject matter. When my students did this project, if I had a particular subject that I wanted someone to research for which there was no reference material available at our school, I would try to find a source of information for the student.

After the first trip to the library and a period of exploring with the opportunity to change the topics, give each student a sheet with the rules and a due date for the finished project. As with other work done during the year it is important that the writing go through several revisions. I would want to see a rough, corrected rough and then the final. On page 59 is a guideline for the project you can personalize and hand to your students.

Below is a sample schedule based on the month of November 98.

Library visit—November 2

All topics picked—November 3

Guidelines handed out—November 4

First draft due—November 10 - 13

Revisions due—November 16 - 18

Turn in project—November 25

Three weeks is sufficient time for this project. Students could use some class time for researching and working in the library. The amount of additional social studies homework should be limited during this project. November works well for a project of this nature, because the project can be due just before the Thanksgiving break. Anyone who has not finished could have the long weekend as a grace period, losing points for being late. If you follow this model, remind your students that they won't enjoy working over the holiday. It might help them get things in on time! This means, however, you have the holiday for grading. Maybe you won't have to cook!

Travel Brochure

This project combines geography, history, current conditions, and includes drawing, writing, and design elements. Begin with a simple discussion about places where students have been on vacation or visited. Did they enjoy the trip? Do they like traveling? What sort of place would be interesting to visit? Did we read about any place in our studies that someone would like to see? Have students brainstorm ideas about historical places that they would be interested in visiting.

Choose a Subject for the Brochure

From ideas generated in the discussion about historic places, each student picks a location about which to create a travel brochure. The brochure will tell the traveler about the physical environment, historical information, and its modern-day advantages.

The research involved differs from that of other projects since students will have to contact airlines, shipping companies, and the consulates of countries where their subject is located for the kind of information that travelers need. To find out more about the history of a chosen location, students could read each other's reports that had been done during the year and research on the Internet. Encourage them to choose places that they don't know much about and might want to visit. Remind them of all they have studied to help them realize that they have the world to choose from.

Write a Proposal

The first part of the assignment is to write a proposal outlining where the student wants to go and why the particular historic site would be interesting to visit.

Format

The format for this assignment should be as much like a travel brochure as possible, including the size and shape of the paper it is presented on. It could include photos or drawings of the historical site, interspersed with text.

57

Information to Include

The travel folder should contain information about the site to be visited including a brief history of the location. The brochure would explain why a visit would be important and interesting. If the subject of the brochure is a new archeological find, some of the reasons why scientists believe it to be a very important and valuable site should be stated. Information about climate and what kind of clothing should be packed for the trip must be included as well as passport information. The vaccinations and other shots that a traveler must have to journey to the location and medicines that would protect his or her health while there would also have to be included. Round trip fares should be added.

I would allow my students to create an imaginary location in a real place for their brochures. For example, students could imagine that something had been found to indicate that Marco Polo had stopped at a place, or that a Viking ship had been found in an area where none had been found yet. If the facts that we studied had made the imaginary event a likely or possible new discovery, I would allow them to explore the idea in the travel brochure.

Because the end of the year has its own excitement, the timetable for this project should be such that the class can share the results of everyone's work. The brochures can be passed around for everyone to read, enjoy, and comment on. Some of the work might be done in the classroom, particularly if there is a good supply of old magazines with pictures that can be cut up for use in the brochures. This project reviews the work of the year and ends the study by seeing some of the old artifacts in a modern setting. It also gives the students a different way of approaching research and sharing the outcome of their work.

This project lends itself very well to development of the presentation on a computer using a scanner, computer graphics and word processing programs, or even a web page if your students are so inclined.

Tip

Ask parents to send in old magazines with lots of photos to use as image and resource material.

Social Studies Research Project Guidelines

Write down the title, author, publisher and date of publication plus specific pages that you have read in every book you have used for information, so that you can list them easily in your bibliography.

Use your notes from the source material as you write your first draft. The revised version or your first draft should be okayed before you start the final draft.

Your final report should be about five pages long (3500 words, typed, 12-point formal font). Include at least two illustrations, in color.

The pages should be secured in a folder or in a cardboard cover secured with paper fasteners. The cover will have the title of your report and your name. You may have an illustration on the cover.

Page 1 – Title Page: title of report & author

Page 2 – Blank

Page 3 – Table of contents

Pages 4 – 10 pages, body of report with 2 illustrations

Page 11 – Bibliography

If you have written more than 5 pages the numbers of your pages will not be the same as those above. However, your first page must be the title page and the last page of your book, the bibliography. The first numbered page will be the first page of your report. If you cannot use a computer, word processor, or typewriter, please see me.

You will have three weeks to complete the project.

- All reading done by _____.

- First draft due _____.

- Corrections to the first draft will be due between the ____ and ___. I will also want to see any sketches or final drawings that you have made for the book.

- Revisions are due _____.

- Final copy is due _____. Check that you have followed all the instructions, that your drawings are finished, your pages in order, and your cover attractive.

If you use a computer, take advantage of the spell check!

Good luck! I look forward to reading it.

TECHNOLOGY

Technology Resources

Software

AppleWorks by Apple Software

Word processing, spreadsheet, database, painting, and drawing programs packaged and interactive together for Macintosh computers

Microsoft Office by Microsoft

Word processing, spreadsheet, database, painting, and drawing programs packaged and interactive together for use by Macintosh or PCs

HyperStudio by Roger Wagner Publishing, Inc.

Multimedia authoring tool

Kid Pix Studio Deluxe by Brøderbund

painting, drawing, animation, and fun stuff

Mavis Beacon Teaches Typing by The Learning Company

Resource Books

Classroom Computer Center Grades 5 and 6 by Concetta Doti Ryan (Frank Schaffer Publications, Inc., 1999)

Making the Most of the One-Computer Classroom by Concetta Doti Ryan (Frank Schaffer Publications, Inc., 1999)

Skills

- Develop standards for interpreting plans and recording data.

- Demonstrate proper use of technology.

- Become familiar with production processes.

- Develop career awareness relating to job applications and forms, types of work and salaries, and association of skills with types of work.

- Develop positive attitudes about work through hands-on building of projects and working with others to develop projects.

- Create and manipulate databases and spreadsheets on the computer.

Since many businesses and service industries use some kind of electronic communication or data processing device, the use of similar machines in school enables students to become familiar with their capabilities. The computer and the calculator, are important parts of our world. Having such devices in the classroom, where they help in the actual learning process, and where students can learn to use them, is important.

Your students need to develop basic skills with the computer keyboard and mouse to speed up entering data. There are resource books to help you learn how to use the computer in your classroom. There are great writing and publishing programs, and database and spreadsheet programs. The media specialist or computer lab teacher of your school or district will help you find good software if you are not sure where to begin.

The computer can inspire the most unwilling writer to write, correct, rewrite, and produce interesting illustrations for written presentations. Since a series of rewrites can be stored or printed, the progress of a piece can be seen easily.

The computer also organizes information in spreadsheets and databases, creates graphs and tables, and can be used as an art tool to create original graphics, and place them into other documents.

The calculator speedily arrives at solutions to mathematical problems. Students must learn the functions of the keys. Getting a quick sum or difference from collected data for a science project, figuring out averages for a chart, and using it as a tool to check pencil and paper work are several classroom uses.

Other useful machines that would be useful for your students to learn about are scanners and fax machines. Scanners assist in converting information on paper to digital (computer) files so that they can be manipulated. Fax machines transmit documents over phone lines.

VISUAL AND PERFORMING ARTS

Visual Art Skills

- Analyze color qualities with distinctions of increasing subtlety such as: hue; intensity; value; and color relationships and harmonies.

- Differentiate objects, forms, and expressions relating to historic periods or cultural origins; materials and processes used; art styles, movements, or periods.

- Identify art principles (balance, unity, emphasis, contrast, rhythm) in natural and human-made forms and works of art.

- Demonstrate an increasing acuity of visual recall in oral, written, and visual expressions.

- Identify implied visual movements such as: direction of a tree limb; sweep of clouds; thrust of a mountain; transition created by the use of line, color, shape, space, and texture.

- Depict the three-dimensional qualities indicated by size, color intensity, overlapping planes, and positions in space.

- Perceive and represent objects from various points of view—from above, below, inside, outside, front, or profile.

- Apply descriptive, metaphorical, and visual art terms to discuss visual and tactile characteristics of objects in the environment and works of art.

- Create in both two- and three-dimensional art forms, with appropriate knowledge of the media and process involved, including: drawing; painting; sculpture; printmaking; photography; collage; and crafts.

- Show confidence in art-making. Demonstrate initiative rather than dependence on teacher direction.

> To give a fair chance to potential creativity is a matter of life and death for any society.
>
> —Arnold Toynbee

- Organize forms thoughtfully in aesthetically pleasing ways, considering line, color, shape, texture, space, contrast, and balance.

- Visualize and use the total area of the working surface, considering both positive and negative space.

- Value originality.

- Express moods and feelings in personal artwork, using art elements and principles.

- Recognize and use a variety of sources of inspiration and content for the creation of art.

- Plan, evaluate on a continuous basis, and complete a work of art.

- Use rudimentary perspective.

- Take care of art supplies and materials.

- Discuss the purposes of art, including: social commentary; celebration; expression of private images; to materialize beliefs and values; to make ideas more understandable.

- Use and evaluate resource materials on art history and appreciation, such as books, periodicals, films, videos, and prints.

- Value and visit collections of original art in museums, studios, and galleries.

- Research and discuss careers in art such as: painter, sculptor, ceramist, craftsmaker, illustrator, photographer, industrial and commercial designer; filmmaker; cartoonist, architect; art teacher; museum educator. Identify and interview artists in some of these fields.

- Explain the contributions of artists to society and the local community.

- Identify the variety of art forms used in business and industry.

- Begin to analyze and discuss ways in which art influences and is influenced by social, political, economic, and technological events.

- Look at and describe visual forms in terms of style and media.

- Compare and describe works of art with respect to: aesthetic meaning; sensory qualities; style; and the materials and processes used to create them.

- Discuss what art is and the aesthetic value of art.

- Compare and contrast artworks of varying styles that depict the same or similar objects.

- Constructively criticize works of art of self and others.

- Demonstrate how design affects function.

Thoughts About Fine Arts

When children begin school they learn using all their senses. When expressing what they have learned they draw, sing, and dance, and sometimes act out a feeling. As children get older they learn to express what they experience in the classroom with writing and reading and working with numbers. They read and write about the things they see in their world and learn to count. Some of the drawing and singing, dancing and acting are still skills used to learn with as they get older. But the opportunities to use an art form to recreate their learning in the classroom diminish as they get older. There is so much to accomplish in school. School boards and parents are not always in favor of sharing the time with the arts, which is why teachers of older children often have to find ways to include some form of artistic expression for their students in the subjects taught in the classroom.

Projects assigned in Social Studies and Language Arts often need drawings to illustrate or decorate some part of a report. The more art experiences that the students have, the more attractive their projects become, and more importantly, the greater appreciation and understanding the students have of the contributions of visual artists to our own and different cultures.

There are schools that realize the importance of the performing and visual arts and provide both the time and space for learning something about them; not only as forms to be appreciated but also as tools for self-expression.

If you are the art teacher for your students because no art specialist is available, don't despair. The art projects I have included here can and should be done more than once, to explore the media. I have also included some art books you can use as references to learn more about teaching the subject.

Line is an identifiable path of a point moving in space. Line can vary in pressure, width, or emphasis. Lines can be gentle, sloping curves; they can be jagged or sharp. Lines may intersect or run parallel. They can begin off the page and end off the page. They may go everywhere!

Shape is a two-dimensional figure identified by a line. Shapes are created by the intersections of lines. They take many forms, such as ovals, circles, squares, or blob-like things! The shape of objects or people in a picture is called the *positive space*; the area around the shapes is called the *negative space*. Both positive and negative space must be addressed by the artist. The positive shapes create the negative space. Ask *What can the artist do to make both interesting?*

Color has three properties:

Hue: The name of the color.

Value: The lightness or darkness of the color. Tint refers to a color's lightness. (Add white to the hue to make it lighter.) Shade refers to a color's darkness. (Add black to a hue to make it darker.)

Intensity: The saturation of the color. (The purity of the color.)

Find a copy of a color wheel so that students may learn about complementary colors (colors opposite each other on the wheel) and adjacent colors (colors next to each other on the wheel). The *primary colors* are **red**, **yellow**, and **blue**. *Secondary colors* are the colors made by mixing two of the primary colors.

Texture is the appearance or feel of a surface that results from the artist's method of using his or her medium.

Overlapping is when an object extends over or rests on top of another object, partly covering it. Put a hat on a student. Discuss what part of the student is hidden by the hat. If students were to draw the head, they would not need to draw the part of the head under the hat. They would draw the brim of the hat meeting the forehead, or eyebrows, or wherever the hat line meets the face line.

For your "studio" sessions (art classes), provide different media and subject matter so that students can experience some of the frustrations and joys of the creative process. They should also look at the work of artists past and present and see the different ways in which those artists interpret their surroundings. Students should experience the importance of visual expression as an important part of our cultural inheritance.

Drawing

To begin an experience in drawing it is often a good idea to show students some examples of that kind of work. If students have been studying Medieval and Renaissance history as my classes did, there will be many examples available from that period. Though drawing is done in many media, start students with pencil or conté crayon because these media are easier for a novice to control.

Experiments with Lines

Your first lesson or as a warmup for the contour drawing lesson, have students fill a piece of paper with varying lines. Use pencil and make them thick, thin, dark, light, straight, curved, jagged, bold, and gentle. Have students experiment with the pressure on their line-making tools to vary the thickness of one line.

> **We have to regard it as our sacred responsibility to unfold and develop each individual's creative ability as dim as the spark may be and kindle it to whatever flame it may conceivably develop.**
>
> **—V. Lowenfeld, "Basic Aspects of Creative Thinking," 1961**

Contour Drawing

Contour drawing is line drawing. It is putting on paper only the lines that can be seen. Discuss what this means, It can be hard for students to grasp this concept. They want to suggest lines that aren't visible from the viewpoint they are using to make their drawing. Another consideration of learning to observe and creating a visual representation of it is how lines appear. The lines we see closest to us are darker, thicker, and more clearly defined than lines that are far away from us. So, on a drawing in which no shading is being used to create the illusion of volume, those parts of the object(s) closes to the eye will be made with a darker line than those farther away from the eye.

A classic contour drawing exercise is for students to draw their own hands. They rest the hands they do not write with next to their paper. They must not move the hand once they have begun. With the other hand they begin to draw what they see, the lines and curves of their hands, never lifting the pencil off the paper. Let students do this slowly and thoughtfully—the finished pictures may not closely resemble hands. That is okay, because the students are learning how to look. Next students draw their shoes. Have students put their shoes on the table and again, looking at the contours, draw the shoes, without looking at their papers, nor lifting pencil from paper. Any object can be drawn this way.

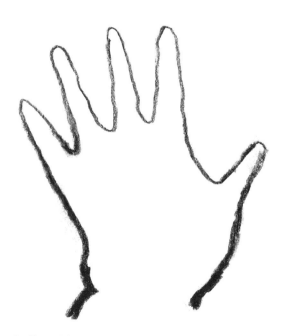

Using Shadows

Provide a simple still life like large geometric shapes, or a long sheet of paper furled around itself. Light it dramatically from one direction (one of the sides will create the best shadows) with a strong light. You could use a table lamp without the shade or a strong flashlight for the lighting effect. You want to create shadows and varying intensity of shadow for the students to recreate in a drawing. You will find that it is easier for a beginning art student to draw a form that is abstract by nature (like a rounded edge of paper) than to begin with an object that the student will want the drawing to resemble.

Volume is different from line in that the farther away from the light source, the deeper the shadow, the darker and thicker the lines and edges the student will make to create the illusion of volume.

After experimenting with the abstract still life, have your students choose a small object to study and draw using line and/or shadows. Possible subjects include a seashell, a leaf, a hat or cap, a stuffed animal, or even a piece of popcorn or a peach pit.

Pulling It Together

Set up a simple still life with jars, a book, and a plant or a pot of flowers. Challenge students to set up their own to combine line, observation, shape, to create a composition with good use of positive and negative space. Have students make two or three sketches of the arrangement of objects with pencil.

Adding Color to the Process

The next step would be to use color in a composition. Show students paintings done by George Bellows, Vincent Van Gogh, Winslow Homer, and Henri Matisse as examples of different ways in which color can be used in a natural setting. If the weather is good, taking sketchpads outside to do some preliminary drawings for paintings to be done in the "studio" (the place where you teach art) will provide students with different subject matter. Sketching outdoors is an assignment that could also be done as homework. Students choose two or three small sketches they are pleased with for the next class. Elements from one or two sketches can be combined to make a painting.

Provide painting materials to students. This project can be done with any paint medium and with chalk or pastel. Students sketch their compositions on their papers and add color to their work. The colors could be naturalistic or imaginative.

Three-Dimensional Work

Visualizing a form in three dimensions and then building it in clay or as a construction using throwaways like boxes and tubes is another test of creative skill.

Learning how to use tools to shape wood can be a very exciting experience for sixth graders and result in useful articles like boxes or wonderful abstract shapes, sanded and polished to a beautiful smoothness. It gives students the opportunity to dominate some very simple tools and to use them to accomplish basic tasks like hammering, sanding and drilling.

Art Field-Trips

Visiting museums to look at work from other cultures and other time periods also helps students to understand and appreciate the importance of artists as contributors to society. Since many trips are planned around a particular curricular goal of the social studies, suggesting to the students that they see the objects that were used not only as relics of the past but as artistic statements gives another dimension to the trip. Take a 9" x 12" piece of cardboard for each student to use as an easel. Attach six or seven sheets of paper to the board with a large paper clip to make an inexpensive and useful sketch pad.

Art Resources

Drawing With Children: A Creative Method for Adult Beginners, Too, by Mona Brookes (J. P. Tarcher, Inc., 1986)

Ed Emberley's Drawing Book: Make a World by Ed Emberley (Little, Brown Publishers, 1991)

Emphasis Art by Frank Wachowiak (HarperCollins, 1993)

Come Look With Me Series by Gladys S. Blizzard (Thomasson-Grant Inc.)—*Enjoying Art With Children* (1990); *Exploring Landscape Art with Children* (1992); *Animals in Art* (1992)

The World of Art through the eyes of artists Series by Wendy and Jack Richardson—(Children's Press, 1991) *Animals; Cities; Entertainers, Families, The Natural World, Water*

Portraits of Women Artists for Children Series by Robyn Montana Turner (Little, Brown and Company, 1992)

Check with the local art museums and galleries to see whether they have an art education outreach program you can use to help you teach art.

Performing Arts

Acting out a situation or role-playing can serve several different needs in the classroom. I have written about the scenes that were improvised in my classroom to enrich our study of the Middle Ages and Renaissance on pages 54 and 55. Though these were not plays in the same sense as studying a script and acting out a story written by someone else, they achieved a similar goal because the acting was done with ease in front of peers. The students were able to pretend to be someone else in a different time period. For our study I felt that improvising was a better method to "write" the stories than putting them down on paper. Having to pretend that you were there as a person, relying on your own words gave the situations a reality that a script didn't and, I think, helped the students learn more about the historic period and also something about performing.

However, memorizing and acting in a play are also very important skills to acquire. Reciting in front of classmates helps to develop the art of speaking in public; practice helps to assuage the stage-fright that most sixth graders have. Important historical documents, poems, and sections from a novel are all written works that can be used to memorize and perform, first in front of the class, then before a bigger audience to help develop self assurance. This oral skill is one to practice in Language Arts since it is a very important part of using language. Reading aloud, reciting, and speaking extemporaneously are all necessary oral skills that can be practiced using writing from the classroom.

Role-playing is an important technique that can be used to help in modifying behavior that has been disruptive in the classroom. Although it uses a dramatic form its goal is not the same. By having two classmates act a scene where a situation is going to result in a hurt, either physical or mental, the class can work out ways in which to avoid a painful situation.

Music Skills

- **Listening**—Identify melodies, scales, rhythms, and specific instruments characteristic of the music of many cultures. Recognize neighboring tones and passing tones. Recognize augmentation (lengthening) and diminution (shortening) as ways of changing patterns of rhythm. Understand forms of musical structure such as *sonata-allegro* and form in larger compositions such as *concerto, opera, sonata, symphony*, and *suite*. Identify chords such as tonic (i), subdominant (IV), and dominant (V) in traditional music and the use of dissonant harmonies in contemporary music. Identify monophonic, polyphonic, and homophonic textures in music. Identify differences in tempo in long compositions. Identify the various vocal ranges. Listen to music with understanding and enjoyment. Identify different styles of music such as classical, jazz, folk.

- **Singing**—Sing several songs independently. Sing the intervals accurately in major and minor scales. Sing songs with changing meters, polyrhythms, complex phrase and section structure, two and three parts, and contemporary devices. Sing expressively with suitable and varied tempos and levels of dynamics. Vary tone quality according to the text of the song.

- **Playing instruments**—Play a minor scale in the key of a familiar song. Play syncopated patterns, changing meters, and polyrhythms on percussion instruments. Play rhythm patterns from songs of many cultures. Play contrasting and similar phrases on bells. Play simple autoharp accompaniments in several keys (*transpose*).

- **Moving**—Learn the traditional conducting patterns for meters of two, three, four, and six. Use movement to represent changes in larger forms of musical structures such as theme and variations. Learn dances representative of various cultures.

- **Reading and writing music**—Understand that a sharp (♯) raises a tone a half-step. Flat (♭) lowers a tone a half step. Natural cancels a sharp or flat.

- **Creating**—Create movements to represent larger structures of music such as theme and variation.

Musical Definitions

Beat: The steady pulse that marks off equal lengths of time.

Tempo: The speed at which a piece of music moves, determined by the length of the beat. Short beats make the tempo fast. Long beats make the tempo slow. "Medium" beats make the tempo moderate.

Melody: A series of pitches and time values that sound one after another. (When you are whistling a tune that you can't get out of your head, you are whistling the melody.)

> **The greatest moments of the human spirit may be deduced from the greatest moments in music.**
>
> —**Aaron Copeland**

Rhythm: The regular recurrence of grouped strong and weak beats in alternation with heavily and lightly accented tones—like the rhythm of the waltz.

Harmony: Harmony is two or more tones that are sounded at the same time. A chord consists of three or more tones sounded simultaneously.

Music in Your Curriculum

Your school or district may provide formal music experiences for students. If not, use the curriculum information listed here to consult with a colleague to discover how music is taught at your school. If you are not musically inclined, and have no colleagues who can assist you to teach music, look to your community. In most places there are musical performers (professional and amateur) who can give you ideas about presenting music. Some may even have the time and interest to come to your class to assist you.

Music of all lands is an important part of our culture and for sixth graders the expressive form that they are probably most familiar with. They all can rap and play air guitar. Some of them may study instruments after school. A chorus and a band may be part of school life, though it is often voluntary and an after school activity.

Playing recorded music in the classroom to compare styles of composers or to inspire writing is a way to incorporate the subject into the curriculum. The pieces played may be the work of composers who lived in the historical period students are studying. Studying different kinds of instruments used around the world and the scale or interval between notes is interesting to analyze in math or science; how it is used in the culture, a part of history and geography. I used music in my classroom as a part of the history study and in our dramatizations.

CHAPTER THREE: ORGANIZATION

THE CLASSROOM

Logistics

Draw an outline map of your classroom on a large piece of paper. Include any immovable and crucial objects on your classroom "map" such as doors, radiators, posts, electrical outlets, the chalkboard, windows, and bulletin boards. Use small pieces of paper to represent desks, filing cabinets, your computer(s), centers, bookshelves, etc. Note on the paper "furniture" any important things to keep in mind as you are arranging the room on paper such as *needs electricity.* Move things around on the map before you move a stick of furniture.

The desk arrangement you choose should be what works best for you. Having desks and chairs that move easily is a wonderful luxury in the classroom because it allows you to group and regroup the students according to what you are doing. Some of the possibilities you have include the following.

- Push two or three desks together so students can share a project.

- Put the desks in traditional rows for test-taking to discourage looking at another person's work.

- Make a circle of chairs for reading or listening.

- Push everything to the back of the room to work on a scene or watch a performance.

Moveable furniture also allows you to put someone who needs your help close to you, or away from a distracting influence.

Because I enjoyed changing the way the room looked, I moved furniture around often and changed peoples' seats regularly. My students didn't object and they did look forward to sitting next to others. One year I tried a lottery every two weeks because I was teaching Social Studies to several sixth grades. I didn't have to assign the seating and if a student wasn't happy for two weeks he or she might be happy with the next draw. A complainer couldn't complain for too long a period! If the class was going to work on projects or do a scene, we would move the desks and chairs to whatever location fit the activity. I usually had my desk at the back of the room; however, I spent a lot of time at the board or in front of the room leading discussions. Sometimes, if someone were absent or there were an empty chair, I sat at a student desk.

Classroom Decor

I started the school year with a big world map on the wall that we could use as a reference. I also hung some museum posters that depicted places that we would be studying. Most of my bulletin boards were used for student work that would be done throughout the year.

Divide the space evenly between the content areas for which you are responsible. You may find it useful to put up some commercial products like a number line or reference charts about subject areas you will be studying to begin the year to personalize the classroom a bit. You could also assign responsibility for organizing and decorating bulletin board space to individual students or groups of students.

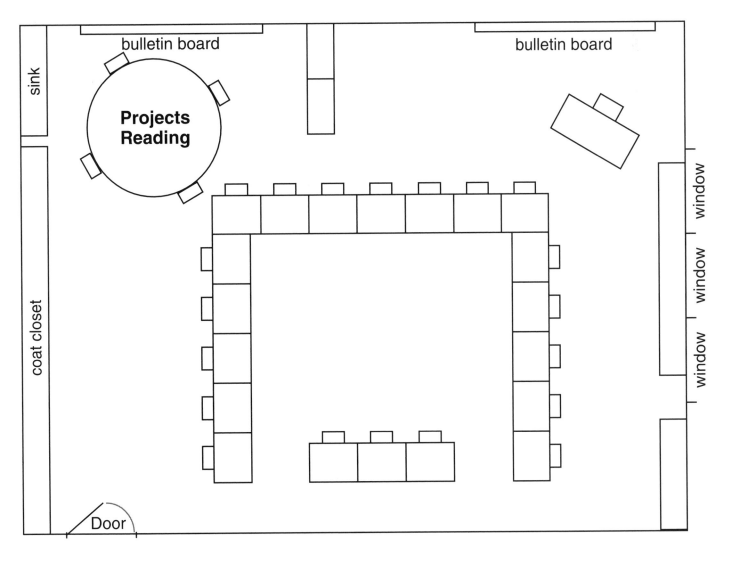

Daily Schedule

Following a daily schedule will make you more effective as a teacher. Schedules let the students know what is coming next, and keep you on track. To make a schedule, start by finding out what times may be planned for you already. Your school may have music, art, or science programs that regularly require students to be away from your classroom. You may be a team teacher with other sixth-grade teachers and the content areas you switch-teach have to be coordinated. Your principal may want to have all students who are in an English Language Development Program to be meeting at the same time. There are usually scheduled recess or lunch times. You may have scheduled yard, bus, or lunchroom duties.

Once you know when students will be with you, divide the day into blocks of time for each subject. Opportunities to read, write, and work with mathematics should occur every day. Your school or district may have requirements about the minimal amount of time that should be devoted to certain subjects. If you have an assistant, consider how you will use her or him during the time assigned to you.

Time	Monday	Tuesday	Wednesday	Thursday	Friday
8:15-8:30	--------Homeroom--------				
8:30-9:15	Language Arts	Science	Language Arts	French	Math
9:15-10:00	Science	French	Math	Science	Language Arts
10:00-10:45	Math	Language Arts	Social Studies	Language Arts	Tech-Fall Drama-Winter Other-Spring
10:45-11:30	Social Studies	Social Studies	Music	Social Studies	Music
11:30-12:15	Music	Math	Library Research	Math	Social Studies
12:15-1:00	--------Lunch and Recess--------				
1:00-1:45	Art	Tech-Fall Drama-Winter	Science lab to 2:00	Art	Art
1:45-2:45	--------Physical Education--------				
2:45-3:15	--------Homeroom--------				

Technology—computers for the fall term-work in the lab honing keyboard skills and learning new computer skills-research on Internet, spreadsheet, graphing, etc.

Drama—for the winter term, could be in conjunction with work in social studies or reading or simply developing skill and ease talking about a subject in front of a group

Other—Individual instrument, independent project, or a special current events study: reading newspapers, discussing TV news coverage

Music elective—brass band or Chorus on Wednesday

Moving Students Throughout the Day

Your school or district may have requirements for how students are to move within the school, so check with your principal. My sixth graders moved from class to class or to lunch, in a rather informal line, sometimes students with partners, sometimes alone. They traveled from class to class on their own. Being quiet so that they did not disturb others who were working was very important, as was staying to the right on the stairs and taking them one at a time. Yelling and running down the stairs were actions that resulted in detentions.

I kept a bathroom pass near the door. A student could leave the room during a study time but not during discussions or class presentations. Only one student could be out of the room at a time so if the bathroom pass was not there, no one could leave for the bathroom. The system worked, although we did have difficulty when the pass was mislaid and something had to be improvised. Since the pass was simply a cardboard disk I embellished with symbols, it was easy to replace.

THE FIRST DAY

Your first day of teaching sixth grade has finally arrived. If you're new to teaching, you are probably as nervous and excited as your students. If you're new to the grade but not new to the school, you may know some of the children in your class by face, name, or reputation. Since this is your first sixth-grade and a new year, you want to get to know them just as they want to get a sense of what you're like on this day.

> Everyone who remembers his own educational experience remembers teachers, not methods and techniques. The teacher is a kingpin of the educational situation.
>
> —Sidney Hook, Education for Modern Man, 1946

You've got a class list and you have gone over the students' permanent records and know about the strengths and weaknesses within the group. But you don't know the individuals or what their particular likes and dislikes are. Suggest to the class that you've all been invited to a social gathering and need to introduce yourself to the other people at the party. Start out by telling them who you are: your name, where you went to school, special things you like to do: work out, read cook books, bowl. You set the pattern; it's an icebreaker. After some volunteered information by a few students and a bit of chit-chat, you hand out a copy of the worksheet found on page 93 to each student.

Personalize the form by asking for odd pieces of information that are not usually requested. Completing the questionnaire will be more thought-provoking and interesting for both you and the students. Later in the year, use a student questionnaire to write a mystery profile, to see how many people in the class know who their mystery classmate is. You will also be able to look over student spontaneous writing to see how well your new students write.

They'll want to know their schedules for the day and the week. Have copies of the schedule available for them. If the school is compartmentalized, students need to know when they change classes and where the classes are. If you teach most of their subjects they'll want to know what the schedule in the room will be like. Will there be a break time? When is lunch? Will they go outside? Do they have gym?

71

STUDENT WORK STANDARDS

Helping sixth-grade students get themselves organized is one of the most basic and important jobs we have as sixth-grade teachers. This organization includes clear communication about homework, explaining our expectations of how work should look when it is turned in, how to take and organize notes, and how to study for tests.

Set up rules for the way papers should look and where they should go when turned in. I suggest that you require a three-ringed notebook to hold 8½″ by 11″ paper. Using dividers to separate subjects, the notebook can be used for all classes. Classwork and homework to be turned in should be written in pen, either blue or black ink. Pencil is to be used for math computations. All papers should have both a right- and left-hand margin.

The advantage of using loose-leaf paper is that work can be turned in, read, and returned to the notebook for study and revision. The disadvantage is the difficulty some students have keeping papers in the notebook. Keep a supply of reinforcements in the classroom and suggest the use of pocket folders to those students whose work spills out whenever the notebook comes out of the book bag. If students are responsible to other teachers for homework assignments, you, as the homeroom teacher, should review the homework load each day. Make one student in the class responsible for writing all assignments on the board so that students can check that they have all their assignments.

Your school or district may have guidelines for what is considered a reasonable amount of homework. If not, an hour plus some reading is a fair amount of homework time for sixth grade. The rule of thumb is 10 minutes per grade level.

> **Nothing is a waste of time if you use the experience wisely.**
>
> **—Auguste Rodin**

HOMEWORK

Provide a Homework Assignment Page (page 92) to your students. Each horizontal band is used for the homework of one subject: language arts, math, science, social studies, foreign language, etc.; the verticals for the days of the week. Parent communications can be written on the back of this form. It is a useful record of work assigned, serves as a way parents can know what their child's homework responsibilities are, and can be used to fill-in someone who has been absent. You might want to consider having students use a separate notebook for the Homework Assignment Page so that it is easy for them to find and keep at the ready.

RECORD KEEPING

Know what records your school and governing agency require, and what records your teaching plans require. Records you may need to keep include daily attendance records, assessment records (including portfolios and test results), lesson plans, permanent school records (usually kept at the school), and homework tracking. Plan your record keeping as soon as you know you have a class.

Daily Attendance

An attendance record is extremely useful. Its obvious purpose is keeping track of attendance, but it has other uses as well. Update this book every day, and keep it close to the classroom exit where it is easy to grab in an emergency. In the event of a fire, earthquake, or other disaster, you need to be able to call roll and check to see that each student is accounted for. If something has happened to prevent you from calling roll, the person in charge of your class will need the information. Even if your school or district has required attendance forms for you to complete, keeping personal records is extremely useful for parent conferences and tracking patterns of absences that may be red flags to other problems the student is facing or help explain poor performance in the class.

Grade Book

You need a grade book. List students' names in alphabetical order. If you have space on the page, leave some blank lines between student names so that you can add new students in alphabetical order when they join your class. Assign different pages in the grade book to different subjects. Ask for a copy of the report card you must fill out for each student, to set up your record-keeping system according to the information you must report. Being in school is directly related to work completed and homework turned in, so keeping the attendance record in the same book as grades may make it easier to correlate the information.

Record grades daily or weekly. Try to keep the paper flowing through your room so you don't drown in it. As you record grades, include information on the grade book that will help you identify the source of the grade when it comes time to do progress reports. For example, in the spelling section you might note at the top of a column of test results, the date of the test and the total number of questions or words included on the test. In a social studies section you might note the name of the project graded and include a column for a content grade, a column for the mechanics grade, and an overall grade. There are computer programs commercially available to assist in keeping grades that make the record-keeping process even easier.

ASSESSMENT

Assessment is an on-going process. You will use several different means of assessment for your students that will include portfolios, tests, quizzes, homework, classwork, project grades, and student evaluations. You will be evaluating daily work, projects, class participation, tests, and homework.

Student Work Portfolios

To keep track of student work, create folders for each student, color-coded for each subject. I used red, blue, and yellow file folders, color-coded by subject (Math, Language Arts, and Social Studies), and posted an index card over the file box that indicated which subject went in which colored file. Keep the box with the folders in a conspicuous section of the room with a section for each student's series of three folders. Keep completed tests, stories, and other writings for the term in the folders. When a test is imminent, students can review the records they keep (their notes and quizzes) and the portfolios. Review work with students suggesting changes to their study habits to improve their performance. You will have to monitor that papers are returned to the correct storage folder.

Creating Tests

Dr. Howard Gardner, a professor at the Harvard School of Education, in the New York Times (op ed page, Friday, December 4, 1998) commented about standardized tests . Dr. Gardner questioned what was being tested and stated that skills aren't being examined. These are the questions that Dr. Gardner posed:

- Does the test focus on something indisputably important?

- Does it test the desired skill directly, or does it use other methods as an index of the student's proficiency (for example, testing students' "writing ability" by asking them to choose the best-written of four sample passages)?

- Are teachers prepared to help students acquire the required skills, and do they have the necessary resources?

- Could students who do well on one test do well on a different sort of exam that presumably tests the same skill?

I think that these questions can be asked about much that we do in the classroom as teachers. Are we really giving our students a desire and love of learning? What is the best way to nourish a student's desire to learn and achieve a high degree of academic excellence? High standards are important and testing to see that your students are working toward attaining them equally so, but study the tests that are given and question what is shown by the scores.

When you create a test about something that you have just covered in class, ask yourself if the question you've asked is the most important thing to remember in that event or story. Are you asking the student to use a skill of thinking or computation that has been taught? Have you prepared them for the test with information and the skill to answer the questions? Do they have the necessary skills to answer questions about the topic that might be put to them by a different teacher?

Project Grades

Assessment of projects and reports has three parts.

- Is the information correct?

- Has the student followed directions?

- Is the material carefully prepared and presented?

Information and presentation were more important to me than following directions. 40%, 40%, and 20% is one way of dividing up the evaluation.

Student Conferences

Student conferences are a vital part of the learning process. Each time a unit is finished and an evaluation made of the student's work on a test or project, discuss the grade with each student individually. When you meet with some students the conference will be a pat on the back, but other students will benefit as you explore with them what the missing ingredient in their learning process was, and what they could do to improve. The list of suggestions for new strategies includes:

- following instructions more carefully

- doing homework in a timely manner

- improving note-taking skills

- using quizzes and tests for review

- asking questions in class when a concept isn't understood

- becoming a more active member of discussions

- keeping the work in their notebook organized and properly filed

The last may be one of the most important strategies that helps students improve their work.

REPORT CARDS

Before you sit down to write your report cards, gather all relevant material—portfolios, your grade book, and anecdotal records. Expect to spend a week or two doing report cards. Some schools and districts provide pre-printed report card forms that you fill in. Others will provide you with blank forms on which to hand write grades that become the permanent report card. It can be useful to make copies of your blank forms—one for each student. You can compile your records on this sheet, and so that any mistakes you make (and you will make some) will be on a non-permanent record which you can then copy correctly onto the permanent record.

Is every grade as important as the others? Some teachers like to drop the worst grade from the student's work and then average the rest of the grades. Others like to weight different work. Keep a detailed grade book set up to coincide in part with the information you need for the report card.

I weighted test scores differently when doing the semester evaluation to determine the grade. Generally I followed this pattern for each subject: 50% of the grade was determined by test scores, 25% from a project score, 15% from quizzes and 10% from the homework score made up the grade. (My homework record was simply plus or minus, turned in or not, half plus if half done etc. I determined their score by dividing number done by number assigned and taking 10% of that. My students were aware that 10% of their grade was whether they turned in their homework or not! I planned a big project, a long novel, and significant writing for each trimester.

Here is another way to weight a grade. Johanna, the sixth-grade teacher, needs to calculate a science grade for Lita Brown. The grades she has recorded for Lita are the following.

Science-fair project - cross-pollinating plants to explore Mendel's plant experiments 5 (out of 5) - or 100%.

Homework assignment - gathering seeds from different plants and comparing them 4 (out of 4) or 100%

Keeping a discovery journal - Lita wrote in the journal extensively every day.

Two in-class science tests 7/10 (7 correct of 10) and 6/9 (6 correct of 9)

Lita participates actively in class.

Johanna could decide that the discovery and exploration aspects of the curriculum are worth 75% of the grade and the tests will be worth 15%, and class participation 10%.

She will figure Lita's grade by adding the exploration and discovery aspects together.

Plant project	100	
Seed homework	100	
Journal	100	
Total is	300 / 3	= 100%

100% of 75 (value for exploration and discovery)= 75 [the equation she used to get this answer is 75 multiplied by 1.0.] As she has 100% in the discovery part of the grade, she will receive the full 75 points of the grade.

Test 1	70%
Test 2	67%
Total is	137% / 2 = 69%

69% of 15 (value for tests)= 10 [the equation she used to get this answer is 15 multiplied by .69] She would receive 10 points of a possible 15 for her tests.

She participates actively in class, so Johanna will give her the full 10 points for class participation.

Lita's total grade is therefore 75 + 10 + 10 = 95.

You can weight your grading system to reflect your curricular goals. Once you have made a decision, treat all students the same way. Make a note of your grade formula for future reference.

Report Card Comments

Many report cards have a section for teacher comments. Draft your comments on a separate sheet of paper before you write them on the final document. Edit your comments for content and mechanical errors. Just as you try to formulate your comments in conference about your students in a positive way, the same needs to be done when you are writing comments that go out with the report cards.

Blunt John never gets his homework assignments in on time.

Better *Although John's homework assignments show his understanding of the subject they are rarely turned in when they are due.*

Blunt Mary's written work is difficult to read because she does not follow the rules of punctuation.

Better *Working on rules of punctuation will make it easier to read some of the interesting papers that Mary has written.*

Blunt Henry's grade on the test is a C- because he did not study.

Better *Henry needs to spend more time preparing for tests so that his grade will better reflect what he is able to do.*

Blunt Alice wastes too much time in class talking about matters that do not pertain to the curriculum. Her work suffers as a result.

Better *Although Alice's concern about her friends' happiness is to be commended, she must remember that study time is not the most appropriate time for discussion of personal matters. Her work needs her full attention to better represent what she is capable of.*

The samples above are simplistic, but give an idea of how one can soften a negative evaluation. Putting the positive first with a qualifier to provide an alternative behavior is constructive criticism. In my experience, only parents read the comments.

To help students understand that the commentary in the report card is as important as the grade, have conferences with them after a marking period and discuss the relation between the two. Plan how to tackle the new term using ideas from the discussion of the past report card. You may be able to teach the student a new strategy for learning.

This is what knowledge really is. It is finding out something for oneself with pain, with joy, with exultancy, with labor, and with all the little ticking, breathing moments of our lives, until it is ours as that only is ours which is rooted in the structure of our lives.

—Thomas Wolfe, *The Web and the Rock*, 1939

CHAPTER FOUR: RELATIONSHIPS

FRAMEWORK FOR INTERACTION

Your relationship with your class and your individual students will be the most important academic relationship you have during the school year. You'll be living and working in the same room for almost ten months. A framework for interaction is needed. You've planned the curriculum, now you need to think about your room as a space in which academic and social interaction will take place.

In most schools, there are school rules and classroom rules. The school administration, teachers, the PTA, and others will have developed the school rules. You and your class will develop the classroom rules. They should be complementary, never contradictory.

School Rules

Moving in the halls and up and down stairs when passing from class to class, eating in the cafeteria, arrival and departure times are the school rules that are usually printed in the school manual and often posted on signs placed strategically throughout the building. Other rules may include that students must stay to the right side of the hall or staircase. They shouldn't run, scream, play tag, or loiter.

77

In the cafeteria, conversation should be conducted in regular tones, food should be eaten and not thrown, students should sit down to eat, throw leftover food into trash cans, and return utensils and empty plates to the proper place. A final category of rules will relate to arrival and dismissal times. There may be a special area where students go when they arrive early in the morning or when their bus arrives and places where they are to congregate at dismissal time either to get picked up by busses, to leave on foot, or to wait for a ride. There may be rules about student presence in the halls before and after school, rain or snow day exceptions, and other nuances particular to your school. Find out what your duties are relating to the release of students at dismissal time. Ask a colleague or your principal to tell you. Check with your principal, administrator, or colleagues to learn how school rule infractions are handled.

Rules are for the safety of all. Even knowing that sixth graders seem to think that rules are made to frustrate them and keep them from getting to their destinations in the shortest possible time. Appeal to their common sense

Classroom Rules

Discuss classroom rules with your students. The rules should include things like "not touching other people's stuff" as well as input from you. They should contain items that preserve the quality of the space such as hanging up coats, keeping papers off the floor, making sure that books on the shelves are arranged in an orderly way, and that chairs are put under the desks at the end of the day. The class would then discuss rules that deal with behavior. The rules should include speaking one at a time (raising hands when the class is having a discussion), respecting the right of others to have different opinions, keeping hands to oneself (no hitting and not going into someone else's desk), being responsible for keeping one's study area in order. No doubt your students will come up with more. Rules don't mean very much if you don't have consequences to help restrain undesirable behavior. It is important that the disciplinary action fit the broken rule. As the class contributed to the list of rules, they should contribute to the consequences.

Some teachers make a contract when the rules and consequences have been agreed upon. The contracts can be individually signed and each student keep his or her copy, or the contract can be printed on a large piece of paper and everyone in the class signs it. If the class has chosen to sign a large copy of the rules, it should be posted in the room. If each member of the class has a copy, there should also be one posted in the classroom in a prominent place. You may want to sign the contract also.

Speaking out, forgetting to push in your chair, not raising your hand might be on a three-times-you're-out basis followed by a consequence such as losing "free time" for a day, having an assigned seat at lunch, or some kind of service such as cleaning a lunch table or straightening up the classroom after school.

PERSONAL CONFLICTS

How conflict is resolved between students depends on what has happened. Sometimes, if the situation seems very personal, it is best to have students discuss the situation by themselves. If they cannot resolve the difficulty, you can sit in as the mediator. If it is a situation that can be generalized such as making fun of someone or "getting-in-their-face", role-playing can be used to help the students see why the behavior should be changed. Role-playing is a technique that helps to equip students with strategies to deal with situations that might come up. The whole class can take part in this as observers to the incident. You should instruct two students to act out a situation. It could be something that happened in the lunchroom. One actor sits down to eat, another comes by and bumps him with his tray. There is food on the tray that gets all over the sitter. The two people involved start to yell at each other and one is about to hit the other when you step in. At this point the action stops and the class begins to discuss what happened. The argument could begin with whether the initial bump was accidental.

Though role playing is a good tool when a situation erupts in the classroom, you don't have time in the middle of an altercation to appoint students to act out a situation. These are the crisis times for which you need to make some kind of plan. Getting the disturbing influence out of the room is one alternative. If your school allows students in the hall, you can send one of the disrupters out of the room while you talk to the other. Then, if you are allowed to leave your class and just be outside the door, you can take that student with you to the hall and discuss the problem with both of them. If you cannot leave the room you must separate the students who are having trouble and talk to each separately, then let the two of them resolve the conflict. Having a cooling-off seat or corner in the room to which a student can retreat before something happens is a good idea. It can be called a safety box or time-out

pen, whatever seems appropriate to the sport's interests of the class.

If there are more than two or three involved in the argument, the work of the class has to stop. At the beginning of the year agree on a signal that means all students must be absolutely quiet, put their heads down on their desks, close their eyes, and count silently to 100.

CLASS SIGNALS

Turning the lights out is a common signal for quiet but it could signal whatever you wanted. Using something like the lights is often more effective than using your voice, but you should think carefully how you want to use it. Just as the fire alarm is an important danger signal, you can decide on one that means instant freeze and pay attention in your room. But it is a good idea to have two distinct signals, one for returning to your seat and being quiet, the other a more important command that will stop everything that is going on in the classroom. Bells, whistles, as well as the room light are all options. One colleague had a Chinese gong to signal stop what you are doing and return to your seat. Find a signal that suits your style and is effective to get the attention of your students, and use it!

> **We have one simple rule here: Be kind.**
>
> **—Sam Jaffe, Lost Horizon, 1937**

SCHOOL STAFF

Colleagues

Although you are directly responsible to your administration for curriculum, record keeping, and everything else that happens in your classroom, your colleagues are the people that you will probably go to most often for help in solving problems and finding out what you should do next. When you begin teaching in a school, they are your most important resource! Some of them will become close friends. If your schedule allows and this is your first year of teaching, observing in another sixth-grade classroom can be very helpful. If yours is the only sixth, go to your fifth-grade colleague and visit that classroom or visit the seventh grade if available. It is interesting to see where your students have been and where they are going. Having your colleague make a return visit, after you are settled in, can help you prepare for an official observation by your supervisor, as well as give you suggestions about working with some of your students and the dynamics in your classroom.

> We might cease thinking of school as a place, and learn to believe that it is basically relationships between children and adults, and between children and other children. The four walls and the principal's office would cease to loom so hugely as the essential ingredients.
>
> —George Dennison, The Lives of Children, 1969

Administrators

Usually the principal of a school is a former teacher who has gone to school to get an administrative credential. In many schools and districts the principal is the person who hires you at a school, while the school employs you. The principal is your manager. He or she is accountable to the powers-that-be and to parents for what occurs in your classroom. Some principals spend a lot of time being educational leaders—keeping in touch with teachers and students, spending time in the classroom and in community areas like the playground or the lunchroom. Other principals focus their energies on running the business side of the school. Their jobs are defined in part by the system in which they work.

As your manager, your principal will observe your work in the classroom. He or she may make an appointment with you to see a lesson or may drop in to see what is going on in the classroom. Formal and informal observations may be noted in your personnel file. If you have a good relationship with your principal, the observations can be a learning experience for you.

In the independent school where I taught, the administrator was called the head. I was responsible to the head of the Middle School. He met with the whole faculty biweekly and also tried to have a biweekly individual conference with each teacher. Weekly lesson plans, difficult students and plans for upcoming events were discussed including any questions that parents might have spoken about to the head.

School Nurse

Many schools and districts have a school nurse full- or part-time. The nurse will coordinate hearing and vision screenings, keep medical information on students with health problems, and often has an office with beds where students who have taken ill can lie down. If you are concerned about a student's health, consult the nurse. He or she may also be able to help you find resources to assist the families of your students who need health care services.

School Librarian

Another important member on the staff of your school is the librarian. Speaking to the librarian about what is available and how he or she prefers teachers to get materials is a way to start a relationship with the library and librarian for you and your class. You should also explore the stacks on your own to see what is there that you'll want the class to use. You need to decide if it is a good room to have students study in. Then you need to ask the librarian if it can be used for research and study and if you have to make a special appointment for your class to be there. Ask the librarian if you can send students on their own to get books. What kind of audiovisual equipment is available?

Custodian

Get to know the custodian(s) of the school. They know where everything is. When you need furniture, special cleaning tools, light bulbs, and paper towels, talk to the custodian. They are powerful. Require students to be responsible for straightening up the classroom at the end of each day. This will make the custodian's job a lot easier, and create an ally for you.

PTA

The PTA is an organization of parents and teachers united to work together to improve the school. The PTA is different in every school. Some are active, some are not. Some will want you to be active in

the organization, some will not. Most PTAs raise funds for special projects that the school has identified as necessary or wanted. Find out what activities the PTA handles at your school. They may have a project that interests you or could directly benefit your class.

FACULTY MEETINGS

Each school has its own meeting schedule. Check at your school to find out about yours. The meetings will cover issues of interest to everyone in the school: presentation of a safety film, basic first aid rules and procedures for the classroom, talks on a variety of subjects concerning acceptance of families with same-sex parents, AIDS-related information, and information from specialists about learning-disabled students. You may discuss procedures for standardized tests, yard duty, current trends in education, and student population.

HOME, SCHOOL, AND PARENTS

Allies or enemies? Parents can be both, but you want them to be your allies. You want them to help you understand their child and make his or her year in your class a productive learning experience.

Back to School Night

The first official meeting with this formidable group comes on Back-to-School Night or Open School. It is early in the year, in September or early October, and is scheduled to introduce you to the parents. Often it is organized so parents have some social opportunity to greet teachers who have taught their children the previous year as well as the principal and other members of the school staff first. After a bit of social interaction there will be a general meeting in the auditorium in which the principal may introduce new teachers or say something about changes and general plans for the year. The parents will then seek out their child's teacher and room. There may be a master floor plan or list that parents can refer to if a general letter for the evening's plan has not been sent out.

If a sixth grader has more than one teacher, a schedule will be posted so parents know where to go when. Because the sixth grade at my school had different teachers for different subjects, we gave the parents their child's schedule to follow for the evening. The meetings were about 20 minutes long, counting the 5-minute travel time! In that way all the teachers got to meet all the parents who had come to the meeting.

As the sixth-grade homeroom and teacher of all or some of the subjects that the student will study, your job is to present the curriculum in the setting that it will be studied by their children. For that reason, one of your first tasks is to set up the room the way you want it to look.

Before the meeting, perhaps with the help of some of your students, you have arranged the seating with names on the desks so the parent(s) can sit in their child's seat. Since you've been in school more than a couple of weeks, there is student work on the bulletin boards along with the posters and map that you put up to start the year. You may know some of the parents because they have come to your room at the beginning of school and introduced themselves, but there will be more that you haven't met. Sometimes the administration of the school will have name tags for parents to put on before they go to their respective classrooms. If not, you can have some already made out, so a parent can pick up the right name tag and put it on when they enter the room. You can then go up to the parent and introduce yourself easily, using his or her name.

Introduction

Your students have probably told you whether their parents are coming so you know when most of your audience is present and can begin. As a new teacher in sixth grade you can start your introduction with a brief account of your experience and education, adding how happy you are to be in this new situation.

Describe the areas of the curriculum that you will be teaching. You may prepare an agenda for parents to follow as you do your presentation. You may have put various textbooks on the students' desks so that everyone has a book to look at as you describe how it will be used. If you have assigned homework reading in one of them, you might explain what your expectations are for that assignment, adding how long you think it should take to do the work. Although notice of materials has probably gone out the first day of school or even before, some of your students may not have what you think is an adequate notebook. You can use this meeting to show the parents an example of the kind that you want the students to use.

Homework

After you have covered all the areas of the curriculum, discuss homework even if you had mentioned it before. Homework will be a direct connection between you and the parent. Since it is such an important part of the learning process, you need to explain to the parents why you give the assignments you do, how much time you expect students to spend on their homework, and how much help they should get from their parents.

Advise parents that the best way to help their children with their homework is to show interest in the subject matter and make sure that their child has a quiet, well-lit place to do homework. Students should be able to do the homework on their own. Explain that if they can't do something then you need to help them in school. If it takes more than an hour to finish an assignment you need to know that too. Helping students understand what they have been assigned so that it can be completed in a reasonable amount of time

is your job. The parents must be made aware that you need to know what students can't do. Then you can work with individuals to make sure that they understand what is in the lessons.

Show the homework communication tool you use to the parents and indicate the space where they can write you notes (page 92). Also let parents know how to contact you. Some teachers give parents their home phone numbers. Other teachers advise parents to call the school, leave a message requesting a return call. The important thing is that parents feel free to contact you if there are problems. Always call back as soon as you can when a parent has left a message for you.

When you have finished describing the curriculum and some of the special things that you will be doing during the year (trips, festivals, class and school parties), ask parents if they have any questions. If some of the questions seem to have more to do with unique qualities or problems their sons or daughters might have, ask them to make an appointment with you to discuss their questions. Your objective on Back-to-School Night is to introduce yourself, give an overall view of the year, and tell parents what your homework expectations are for them and the students. Your time with parents will go fast, so keep your objective in mind as you talk.

> We become not a melting pot but a beautiful mosaic. Different people, different beliefs, different yearnings, different hopes, different dreams.
>
> —Jimmy Carter, speech, Pittsburgh, Pennsylvania, October 27, 1976

> I've come to the frightening conclusion that I am the decisive element in the classroom. My personal approach creates the climate. My daily mood makes the weather. As a teacher, I possess a tremendous power to make a child's life miserable or joyous. I can be a tool of torture or an instrument of inspiration. I can humiliate, humor, hurt, or heal. In all situations, it is my response that decides whether a crisis will be escalated or de-escalated, a child humanized or dehumanized.
>
> —Haim Ginott

Parent Resources

At the end of your presentation you can mention which events you are planning that need parent volunteers. Have index cards prepared and ready for parents to fill in that night. There should be a line for name, home and business telephone number and a "can-do" area, with a place for days and hours of availability. Try to get the group to finish filling out the cards before they leave so that you have an idea whom to ask to help in the classroom.

Many parents, whatever their fields of work, have something of interest that they might bring to the classroom for special talks or demonstrations. You could ask for this on the index card, too. Pursue details in a phone conversation or during conference time. You may need volunteers for trips as well and this is another category to include on the card.

If there are special community programs in the school available to students and parents, you may want to talk about them at the end of the meeting. Special tutoring sessions, learning a musical instrument, chorus, arts and crafts programs, 4H Club and Scout meetings might all take place in the building after school.

Parent/Teacher Conferences

Formal Parent/Teacher Conferences with the parents or caregivers of every student in your class are scheduled after report cards have gone out so you can share with the parent some of the classroom work that supports the evaluation that you have made. Parent/Teacher Conferences are a very important part of teaching. Just as a homework assignment helps to keep the parent abreast of what the student is doing, the conference helps to describe how everything fits together and explains the evaluation on the report card. If the year has gone along normally and the student has been working to his or her potential, this will be the first meeting with the parent since Back-to-School Night. You are going to talk about the student and his or her work. Prepare for all Parent/Teacher Conferences by having the student work files ready and at hand, your grade book, and any other information that you will need as a reference.

Students Who Are Doing Well

The conference about students who are doing well goes easily. You will have pulled from the student's various files work that is representative of his or her overall accomplishments. Good work that shows the student's potential should be shown first, because it is the high mark you know he or she can achieve and should be the goal for all the work to be completed in the class. You might also show an example of a paper that was not up to the expected standard as a result of an absence, but explain that the mediocre performance was rare because the student made up missed work easily. This can help to reassure the parent that you are aware of the ups and downs of the student's life and are not pressuring the child. The examples of the student's work that you show the parent support the evaluation on the report card. Recounting an anecdote in which the student helped someone in the class, shared with a classmate, or some other out-of-the-ordinary incident during the school day helps to complete the picture of the student as a whole person.

Students on the Border

When you have a conference with the parent of a student who is just on the border, whose work hasn't been so poor that you've felt it necessary to have a pre-report card conference, the conference may be more difficult. This student reads with understanding, joins in discussions with excellent ideas, and is a good problem solver. One project was beautifully done. The student shows a genuine interest in the work of the class. However, since homework is not completed in a timely manner and much of the written work is messy because it has often slipped out of the notebook and gotten filthy from sitting on the floor, his or her grade is lower than it should be. It is the every day work that does not get the student's full attention. Discussion with the parent should center on what will best help this student to achieve what he or she can as demonstrated by oral contributions, general enthusiasm, and a beautiful project. Getting parent support for a better-supervised homework time and some help monitoring the organization and condition of the student's notebook will be helpful. Coming to an agreement about what both home and school can do to help the student gives the conference a positive ending.

Students Having Difficulties

The most difficult conference is about the student who has had trouble since the beginning of the year. In spite of the early conference advising the parents about their child's difficulties and the extra support that he or she has had both at home and in school, there has been no improvement in the child's work. The discussion at this conference will be about the kind of help program that can be set up for the student. Your supervisor or learning specialist may join you in the discussion. Since the parents have been involved since the beginning of the year, the decision to seek outside help will not be so devastating. However, it will not be an easy conference. You need to show as many examples of the student's work as you can collect for the parents to look over as well as a great deal of compassion to come to an agreement about what is to be done.

Each conference should help you understand your students better because you learn something about parental expectations. The conference also gives you the opportunity to communicate with parents about the student's relationship with peers, strengths that may not be reflected on the report card (intellectual, interpersonal, and intrapersonal) and social development as a responsible citizen.

CHAPTER FIVE: CLOSING THOUGHTS

will remember it best if they hear the information accompanied by music. Help your students find the best way that they organize and learn.

HELPING STUDENTS LEARN TO GET ORGANIZED

I cannot overstate the importance of helping students learn to organize and take notes. Review outlining forms. Review how to make outlines. Regularly discuss how to organize material that the students need to learn. As a class, develop different ways to organize material. Some students will remember things written down, others need to draw pictures. Some students will need to do some physical action to remember information, others

FIELD TRIPS

Trips that enrich the curriculum need special preparation, including previewing the location. Transportation, public or private, permission slips, notifying the cafeteria, arranging for bag lunches to go, and collecting money for admissions are things you may have to take care of. You need to know what health forms you are required to have with you (frequently required are authorizations to treat a child in the event of a medical emergency), whether permission slips are required, and what to do with students without signed permission slips. Finally, check with the office or school nurse to see whether you must take a first-aid kit with you.

ENGLISH LANGUAGE DEVELOPMENT

In your sixth grade there will be students of different abilities, but within a normal range of competence. There will also be some students who do not fit into the normal range because English is their second language or they have a learning deficit that has kept them from learning even if the techniques employed in your school are multi-modal and hands-on. The student may need a quieter environment, a more kinesthetic method of learning, special tutoring or simply time to absorb what has gone on in the classroom. Often children who are disabled or learning English as a second language will spend some time out of their regular classrooms.

How to include them in the daily activities of your sixth grade so that they feel a part of the class is the question that you must deal with. One way of accomplishing this difficult task is to modify the assignments for these children: not as many spelling words, writing a paragraph instead of a page, doing seven problems instead of ten. Speak slowly and clearly to the non-English speaking student. Appoint a peer mentor to buddy with the student to help with understanding the things that are needed on class, and to take around the school and introduce to others. If there are others in the class who share the same background and have a better understanding of English, they can act as translators. If there is no English Language Development program in your school, you may want to suggest tutoring to the parents.

However, students who speak another language whether Spanish, Mandarin, Japanese, French or Russian should not be made to feel that they must give up the language of their culture for English. Whatever the program is called to teach students English (Bilingual, Immersion, Dual Language) it should not be an exchange of one language for another. Honoring the first language of the student is also a way in which another culture, something different, is honored. All students in the class should show respect for other languages and the people who speak them.

LEARNING DISABLED STUDENTS

Learning disabled students are often at a great disadvantage. Even though they speak the same language, are often very bright and look like all the other people in the class, they don't act like their peers. They are demanding and may act out and disturb the rest of the class because they are frustrated. Finding the way to include them in class activities so that other members of the group are accepting of their efforts takes patience from everyone. Again, making their assignments shorter or giving them a longer time to accomplish the tasks is helpful. Incorporating something that they do very well such as drawing or playing an instrument as part of one of the scenes for the social studies play includes them. Giving an oral report instead of a written one is another way of describing the information they found for their research project.

Make sure the students with special needs understand their assignments and write them down correctly in their assignment books. They may need help understanding the sequence in which work should be done, since this, too, is an area that can cause trouble.

Be sure that you know when your students are supposed to take medication as this can often have a dramatic effect on their behavior. Staying in touch with the parents of these students who have special needs is very necessary. They can advise you when changes in medication take place and share other important medical information with you.

> **I expect to pass through life but once. If, therefore, there be any kindness I can show, or any good thing I can do to any fellow being, let me do it now, and not deter or neglect it, as I shall not pass this way again.**
>
> **—William Penn**

INCLUSION

As teachers and as human beings we also have to be sensitive to many issues. The issues of the place of the physically- as well as mentally-disabled student in the classroom, how the non-English speaking student should learn in the classroom, and how classes should be organized without excluding anyone because of race or national origin. Each school system operates in the best way it can to be inclusive. As a new teacher you have to see how you can bring that inclusiveness into your own classroom.

SUBSTITUTE TEACHERS

Ask your principal or school administrator what to do when you are out sick or have an in-service that will take you off campus on a school day. I think it is fair to say, without demeaning the substitute teacher and his or her work in the classroom, that when you are out a day or two, not all you hoped will get done. Sometimes not even what you had carefully written out in the lesson plan for substitutes will have been accomplished. Do not be surprised; the substitute may have seen a wonderful teachable moment. Hopefully, whoever took over for you will leave a note about what was accomplished.

The following is a list of ideas for things that you should include in a SUB PACKET that will be found easily by the person who is coming to take your place. Your school may have a form that you fill out that is given to the Sub by the school secretary or receptionist. However, some note from you may give the new teacher more confidence about working with the class if they find some of the information below. The purpose is to give that other person a road map so he or she doesn't get lost, or lose the class during the day, and should minimize the possibilities of torture by your sixth graders! Remember what you use to do when there was a sub?

1. Have a class list and a seating chart in your plan book or on the wall near your desk to facilitate taking attendance and knowing the names of the students.

2. Note where the Fire Drill rules are posted.

3. Note where the weekly schedule is posted. Leave directions as to routes your class takes to get to different areas in the school: cafeteria, library, recess area, gym, auditorium.

4. Special notes about students: those who have to leave to go to special classes and when, someone who will most probably try and get away with mischief, a student who will be helpful, and a student with a medication schedule.

5. Rules for leaving the room, especially to go to the bathroom.

6. An outline of specific work the class should finish during the day. A suggestion for an activity to introduce to the class instead of the expected. It could be a puzzle, a contest, a game or a drawing experience. *Heads, Bodies, and Tails* is fun. Fold a half sheet of paper into three parts. Have the first person draw a head in the top section of the paper with two lines extending a short way into the second section and then fold the first drawing leaving the two line ends visible. The second person connects to the lines and draws an upper body leaving two lines extending into the third section, then folds the paper under a second time so both parts of the drawing are hidden. A third person finishes the drawing with the bottom part of a body (which may or may not include legs!) Unfurl the drawings and hang them on a board for all to enjoy. They could be colored to finish the project.

7. Leave the name of a colleague who knows your kids and will help the teacher fill in the blanks such as where the adult bathroom is located, if there a Faculty Room, and where to find the phone!

RESOURCE TEACHERS

There are many people essential to the smooth running of a school. However not every school has everyone that it needs. Often those who are certified teachers of the learning disabled go from school to school doing diagnostic work and helping teachers who have problems with mainstreamed students in their classrooms. Learning about the different methods that one can use with children who take in information in very unique ways is one of the areas of expertise that a Resource Specialist in Learning Disabilities can offer the classroom teacher. It would be very helpful to you if such an expert could visit your classroom and, after an observation, discuss what you can do to improve the classroom experience for everyone, those who have been diagnosed with learning disabilities and those who have problems within the normal range. The specialist may also come up with suggestions as to how the various styles of learning can be integrated.

Whether you have one or several students mainstreamed in your class you need special advice and support. It is available, but you have to find out how to get it for your particular classroom in your particular district and state.

Independent schools as well as public schools may have a reading teacher on the staff who works with students who need special help. The recommendation for help is made by the student's teacher to the head of the division or supervisor, followed by a conference with the parents informing them that the extra help is available and will assist the student in conquering difficulties he or she is experiencing. Some parents will choose to hire specially trained tutors to come to the school to work with their child. However the help is made available to the student the goal is to enable him or her to develop their skill in reading in order to be able to work independently.

In society today we have a large group of children who are labeled learning disabled and it seems to be growing. What has caused this increase is

> Teaching is a moral calling, a craft, and an intellectual occupation. It is often values that bring one to education in the first place. The craft develops through experience and reflection upon that experience. What is hardest to maintain in the midst of the immediate demands of the classroom is the intellectual aspect of teaching, which, though less apparent on an everyday level than the craft issues, still pervades and underlies every good teacher's practice. It has to do with teachers' analysis of how children learn, of the role of ethnicity, gender, and class in learning, of the relationship between school and society, and of the translation of moral values into specific classroom practice.
>
> —Herbert Kohl

difficult to determine, but the changes in family structure, crowding in urban areas, and TV as a baby sitter are probably all part of the problem. As a teacher in the classroom you can offer as much support as possible to each of your students by giving them individual help. If the student is not succeeding in the classroom, you can recommend that he or she be tested or given special tutoring.

CHILD ABUSE

In many places, teachers are required by law to report suspected abuse to the social service agencies. The procedure may be to report it directly to the Agency, or through the school. Check with your principal about how it is handled at your school.

PHOTO RECORDS OF THE YEAR

You and your students will enjoy seeing a photographic record of the year. Bring your camera to school! On the first day of school I tried to have everything ready so that I could "shoot" the students as they came into the room for the first time and I got some nice candid shots to put on our door to identify the room and make it ours. Since getting double prints of a roll of film didn't cost more, I gave the double to the student whose picture it was. It was a nice introductory gesture.

I did not take photos every day but tried to keep a record of important happenings in the classroom and trips. Photographing the students working on projects and their displays at the end of that hard labor as well as rehearsals and final productions of class plays made wonderful remembrances of the year. Your school may have cameras or video cameras available to loan to you for use in the classroom.

GENDER ISSUES

I have always used the term *man* in the sense that it means humanity, and the Latin classification Homo sapiens in the same way. In the last ten years, I have had to be careful when I spoke about *Early Man* or *Medieval Man* in my history classes. At the beginning of the year the sixth-grade girls always caught me with a question about women. Where were the women, were there only men then? This made me realize that I had to correct my old ways and use inclusive nouns, gender-general ones or his/her in my writing and talking. If you are interested in exploring the issue of gender equity in the classroom, you will find information on the World Wide Web about it. The keywords to use are Gender Equity.

DISASTER DRILLS

Disaster drills require a safe, quick and quiet exit from a building. The special rules for lining up, going down the stairs and exiting the building should be reviewed in the first week of school in preparation for a drill since they are different from the day-to-day passing from class to class. The students should be reminded of the importance of the drill, particularly the rule about talking. Quiet is necessary so that everyone can hear all instructions whether they come from a teacher, an administrator, or a firefighter. If you are a new teacher to the school, practice disaster drills with your class at the beginning of the year.

SELF-EVALUATION

Self-evaluation is a valuable exercise for improving our performance as educators. Find a colleague who would like to partner with you in the process, someone who you trust. Set a time when he or she can observe and take notes on you giving a lesson to your class. After the lesson, arrange a conference for the follow-up. Your colleague will meet with you and share the notes and his or her conclusions. The things that your colleague saw can be interesting and useful. He or she may have noticed things that you couldn't see because you were at the board and did not have an open view of the whole room. Ask questions of the observer. There are advantages to experiencing interchanges like these, not the least of which is that you will be better prepared for a formal observation by the principal. You will also have the opportunity to observe your partner teacher in action. You can both learn a lot about being more effective teachers from each other. The exchange you have with your colleague is not a theoretical discussion nor a textbook example. The classroom experience is authentic.

It is a great help to your teaching if you can do this kind of peer sharing. It is a great help to have someone see what you do and understand it. We teachers don't get a lot of appreciative pats on the back. And, as in any profession, the professionals know where the difficulties are and appreciate most how someone overcomes them. You and your partner teacher will be exchanging the pats on the back that you both deserve.

EPILOGUE

I would like to include my thanks to everyone who helped me put this book together. My colleagues Fran Warner and Steven Schwartz; Anne, who trusted me to help her through her first year; Willie Krabor, who was my first mentor many years ago; my neighbor, Julie, the computer guru; and Barbara, an editor who has infinite patience. These are just a few of the many people from whose experiences I profited.

This is the end of *Getting Ready to Teach Sixth Grade*. You are now all set to begin in your new classroom! I hope that you will find that my ideas and words of experience may be of help to you. Using an idea from this book and giving it your own twist will be the utmost compliment to everyone who had a hand in putting this book together!

Have a wonderful time with your class. I am sure they'll give you as much as you'll give them!

Every second we live is a new and unique moment of the universe, a moment that never was before and never will be again. And what do we teach our children in school? We teach them that 2 and 2 makes 4 and that Paris is the capital of France. When will we also teach them what they are? We should say to each of them: Do you know what you are? You are a marvel. You are unique. In all the world there is no other child exactly like you. In the millions of years that have passed there has never been a child like you. And look at your body what a wonder it is! Your legs, your arms, your cunning fingers, the way you move! You may become a Shakespeare, a Michelangelo, a Beethoven. You have the capacity for anything. Yes, you are a marvel. And when you grow up can you then harm another who is, like you, a marvel? You must cherish one another. You must work—we must all work—to make this world worthy of its children.

—Pablo Casals

91

Homework Assignments

Name _____

Week of	Monday	Tuesday	Wednesday	Thursday	Friday
Subject _____ _____ _____	_____ due _____	_____ due _____	_____ due _____	_____ due _____	_____ due _____
Subject	_____ due _____	_____ due _____	_____ due _____	_____ due _____	_____ due _____
Subject	_____ due _____	_____ due _____	_____ due _____	_____ due _____	_____ due _____
Subject	_____ due _____	_____ due _____	_____ due _____	_____ due _____	_____ due _____
Subject	_____ due _____	_____ due _____	_____ due _____	_____ due _____	_____ due _____
Subject	_____ due _____	_____ due _____	_____ due _____	_____ due _____	_____ due _____

FS122008 Getting Ready to Teach Sixth Grade

Student Profile

Name _____

Address _____

_____

Date and place of birth _____

_____

Color of eyes _____

Affix student photo here.

The student pictured above is most likely to _____

_____

_____

Number of siblings _____ Names _____

Favorite sports: as spectator _____

Favorite pastimes _____

Pet Peeve _____ Favorite subject in school _____

Least favorite subject in school _____ Favorite color _____

Goal at 18 years _____

Goal at 25 years _____

Favorite food _____ Favorite Singer _____

Write a paragraph about what you did this summer. Include a self-portrait.

_____

_____

_____

_____

Award Certificate

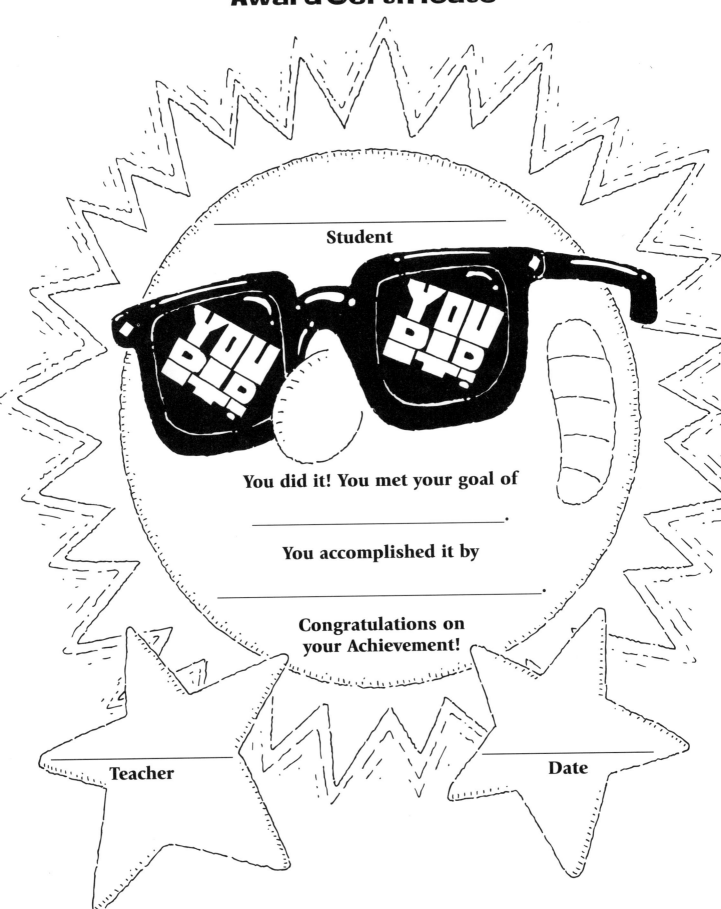

Student

You did it! You met your goal of

_____.

You accomplished it by

_____.

**Congratulations on
your Achievement!**

Teacher

Date

94